OFF THE RECORD COLLECTION
Riffs, Rants and Writings about Rock

OFF THE RECORD COLLECTION

Riffs, Rants and Writings about Rock

James VanOsdol

Haaf-Onion
Chicago

First Haaf-Onion edition June, 2011
ISBN 978-0615454962
Published by Haaf-Onion Omnimedia
http://www.haafonion.com

This book is respectfully and lovingly dedicated to my wonderful wife, Anne, and my amazing children, Noah and Fiona.

If not for them, my life would be a sloppy tragedy of Fritos, Jack Kirby comic books, and failure.

ACKNOWLEDGEMENTS

Once I'd made the emotional leap and committed myself to publishing this book, I realized that I needed help.

I'd like to use this space to formally thank John Tomkiw for creating this book's magnificent cover and jacket. John's a gifted writer, artist, and overall creative force. I truly don't deserve his generosity.

The book you now hold in your hands was made significantly better because of the feedback, suggestions, and support I received from valued friends like Mike Englebrecht (welcome!), Mike Bratton, Patrick Brower, and Sandra Madison.

Traditional publishers have long insisted that celebrity endorsement "blurbs" are important to help sell a book. From what I understand, they're meant to make the casual reader think "hey, cool people are into this, what the fuck am I waiting for?" Knowing that, I enlisted some very cool people to lend me their quotes and quips: Bill Leff, one of the funniest people in the history of Chicago media; Tim Seeley, one of the 21st century's most exciting comic creators (and no stranger to creator-owned material); eternal nice guy and talented artist Tony Akins, whose work on *Fables* and *Jack of Fables* made those monthly stories jump off the printed page; and old friend/world-renowned Styx drummer Todd Sucherman. I've been a fan of Todd's for the better part of the past 30 years; he remains virtually peerless in the world of rock drumming.

On a final note, I'd like to thank my parents for always encouraging me. Sorry about the profanity in the pages that follow, Mom and Dad.

CONTENTS

INTRODUCTION

Life is a series of critical responsibilities: school, work, marriage, and parenthood. How we handle these commitments defines our emotional and professional health and happiness. In short, these are the things we can't fuck up.

To balance out our most weighty and mature priorities, we humans find diversion in recreational pursuits and activities. For some, the recreational balance is struck by participating in sports. For others, it's found in hookers and booze.

I write.

I wouldn't say I write for fun, and I definitely don't write for money (which isn't for lack of trying, mind you). I write because I have to.

Let me say that again, this time with emphasis: *I write because I have to.* For as long as I can recall, writing's been my way of finding peace and release. It's my touchdown throw, late-night jog, and callgirl all in one. Best of all, I can walk away from a night of writing without dropping a bead of sweat or catching Chlamydia.

Most nights, it doesn't matter what I write. I've written a landfill's worth of awful material—bad fiction, mean-spirited critiques, maudlin stories about my kids—that no one ever needs to read. The goal was never to have anyone read that material, of course; I wrote it because I had to.

On the other hand, there are those things I've written that people can, and have, read--blog entries, mostly. Some newspaper, magazine, and online articles, too. The problem has always been that, once I send those writings out into the digital wilderness, they never come back home.

Blogs march on, their entries only truly mattering during a brief window of SEO-enhanced findability. As more writings stack up, older entries get pushed further back into obscurity, making a case for electronic Natural Selection. Old blog entries and online articles are timestamped snapshots of a bygone time, and in the internet age, a bygone time can be as recent as two years ago.

In late 2010, I decided to drop an anchor into the timestream and gather my writings into a net. I wanted to provide order and context to the things I've said and written in the 21st Century. And then what? I wondered. I wanted to have the collection published, but didn't want to spend months navigating around the traditional publishing idiom of finding an agent, sending query letters, and mailing out hard copies of the manuscript. The solution was obvious: I'd publish the book myself.

The internet age has made the notion of "D.I.Y." publishing a surprisingly easy proposition. With limited resources and a fair amount of commitment, anyone can self-publish their work, regardless of that work's quality, intended audience size, or marketability.

The "Publish on Demand" model has long been stigmatized by critics and the literati, despite the fact that going "D.I.Y." is a sign of ethical purity in practically every other art form. In the music world, for example, independent music is treated as honorable and "real." Major label, "professional" releases are perceived in quite the opposite way: vastly inferior to indies and most likely ethically and artistically compromised.

Along the lines of music-centric publishing, what would music criticism have been without the D.I.Y. 'zine culture that informed the underground's opinions in the '80s and '90s? I know I enjoyed *Punk Planet* and *Tailspins* in the '90s more than I ever did a single issue of *Rolling Stone* or *Spin*.

None of this is to say that what I've written here is ethically pure or high art. It is, however, said to make the point that there's nothing inherently wrong with creating something and managing every step of its release into the world, which is what I've done here.

In order to self-release this collection, I created a name for my publishing company (Haaf-Onion), and began sequencing, editing, and formatting the manuscript that became this book.

For this volume, rather than include everything I've ever written, I decided to piece together content specific to one overarching topic: Music.

Included on the following pages are blog entries, tweets, interviews, shelved concepts, and excerpts from a never-published book of mine called *Chicago Rocked*. The contents are far from everything I've written about music, but they're enough for the purposes of this book.

One of the downsides in self-publishing is that the burden of editorial direction and correction has been my own. I claim full responsibility for bland and/or clichéd writing, shitty grammar, misspellings, and syntax WTFs you may encounter. Flaws aside, I take pride in the fact that I was able to create something coherent, self-publish it, and get it into your hands.

I've made minor tweaks, mostly spelling, punctuation, and modest rephrasing, to previously-seen material. Rather than completely rewrite old content, I wanted to present it in the way it was originally written. It seemed dishonest to completely alter it.

Even so, the decision to keep the older content intact wasn't an easy one. That awkward feeling you get when you open an old high school yearbook and realize that the dork with a bad haircut is you? That's how I felt as I was digging through my archives. What I saw was definitely *me*, but it was a "me" from the past. My writing's matured over the years, but the essence of those earlier works is still uniquely my own.

Thank you for buying *Off the Record Collection*. Now that we've made it this far together, we may as well be friends:

james@jamesvanosdol.com
(Twitter) jamesvanosdol

Sincerely,
James VanOsdol
Chicago, Illinois

OLD WAVE: NOSTALGIA

CHAPTER ONE

My experience has found that people create their most meaningful and lasting music attachments with the artists and songs they grew up with. That's not to say that such attachments can't happen later in life; it's just that there's something special and deep-rooted about connections made during the teenage years.

I graduated high school in 1987, and my music comfort zone completely falls in line with the albums and songs I listened to during my senior year. That comfort zone finds me making excuses for music I should know better than to support: Phil Collins' No Jacket Required? *Love it. Can't get enough of those Peter Gabriel backing vocals on "Take Me Home." "Video Violence" by Lou Reed? Sure, it's no Velvet Underground; and, granted, it's only a bit less laughable than* Metal Machine Music, *but what a charming, topical, track from Mr. Waiting for His Man...*

While I've always tried in my adult years to be aggressive about seeking out new music, I can't help but fall for the nostalgia of my youth.

And I know I'm not alone.

(July 17, 2010)

<u>The Case for Nostalgia-Cheap Trick and Squeeze</u>

I've been to (outdoor concert arena) Ravinia less than five times in my life, primarily due to lack of interest in the artists that are booked there (sorry, Bo Deans). Besides the bookings, I also have no interest in the overall Ravinia vibe: competitive picnicking done by rich douchebags getting loaded on wine, trying to relive their high school days. Cheap Trick was enough of a reason for my wife and me to venture to Ravinia last Saturday night.

We don't have the mettle for competitive picnicking, so we opted for pavilion, rather than lawn, seats for the show. The pavilion is a much better call, anyway, seeing as the volume is much quieter at Ravinia than all other outdoor rock venues. That's what you get for dropping a live music venue in a pricey suburban 'hood.

Squeeze opened the show, smartly shelling out the complete track listing of *Singles 45's and Under*. I've seen Squeeze a few times in my life, and there should be no surprise that they sounded better, performed better, and were more meaningful in their 80s heyday. On stage at

Ravinia, the band looked bored as they coughed up literal recitations of the dated-sounding material. On a related note, holy hell, their music does not stand the test of time. During the show, I saw people my age--people who were probably at the same Poplar Creek show I saw in the 80s--convincing themselves that they were having fun, bouncing around to "Cool for Cats" and the like. They had tricked themselves into thinking the band on stage was anything more than the dullards they were. The crowd had a desperation for reliving the past that defied what their senses should have been telling them. That's nostalgia for you--the burning need to relive a memory in exactly the same way it was once experienced.

Squeeze performed for 75 minutes, which was about 40 minutes longer than what it should've been (I learned after the fact that they were co-headlining the show). In no universe or concert line-up should Squeeze ever again be allowed that opportunity.

In stark contrast, with their "big rock show" stage set-up, larger-than-life personalities, and overall sound, Cheap Trick took command of the stage from the second they hit it.

Robin Zander's voice has made it through the decades without a crack, fissure, or break in intensity or range. He absolutely nailed the set-opening "Way of the World," a song that swept into two more barnburners, "Come On, Come On," and "I Want You to Want Me."

Unfortunately, spinning out of that initial, triumphant, triumvirate of songs was an awkwardly-paced and tough-to-sit-through setlist. Take, for example, "Heaven Tonight," the title track from the band's 1978 classic. On disc, it's a plodding oddball piece of psychedelia; in concert, it's a momentum-killing cue for a bathroom break.

The concert was loaded with five songs from Cheap Trick's most recent album (the poorly named *The Latest*), a mostly unmemorable release. I tried to love the new songs live--I swear I did--but it just wasn't happening for me.

As I watched Cheap Trick play their new songs, I gave them credit for not allowing themselves to be a nostalgia act. Unlike the majority of their 70s-spawned peers, Cheap Trick isn't coasting on their greatest hits (though I would've killed a drifter to hear "She's Tight").

To summarize the night, Squeeze played like a street festival-headlining nostalgia act. Having lived through the band's initial run, their entire performance made me feel old.

And while I didn't love Cheap Trick's set, their performance resonated more as an uneven show from an otherwise great band. Sure, there was nostalgia to squeeze out of the timeless tracks they did play (e.g."Surrender," "Baby Loves to Rock"), but nostalgia never once defined the show.

And there's the message: you can celebrate your past without being defined by it. Thanks, Cheap Trick.

In January, 2011, I was invited to participate in an ongoing spoken word event called "First Time." As it was explained in a press release:

"The First Time is CHIRP's (Chicago Independent Radio Project's) reading series that combines the written word and music. Local musicians/performers/writers write and read an original piece based on a 'first time' theme. This month, we're featuring 'First Car.' The piece will reference a specific artist or piece of music, and immediately following, a live band will perform the aforementioned song. This is a benefit for the Chicago Independent Radio Project.'"

The idea of doing spoken word was out of my comfort zone, which is what made me think I should do it. I wanted to know if I could pull it off. Besides, the event was planned to be held at one of my favorite music rooms in Chicago, Schuba's.

Instead of sharing stories about my first car, I focused on my music-listening habits in high school. Here's my script, which I somehow managed to memorize and deliver without awkward stammering or nervous fast-talking.

(January 26, 2011)

First Time: Keys to the Tape Deck

I was raised as a Jewish boy in Skokie--I'm really not a car guy. And that begs the question: Oh my God, what am I even doing here?

I was in high school when I got my first car. Niles West. Go Indians.

My first car was a boat. A total beater. A used '76 blue Monte Carlo. I'm sure that my parents thought it was the type of car that could withstand weekends of abuse from my dumb buddies and me.

My strongest memories of the car had nothing to do with the mechanical aspects of it. I couldn't tell you what I had under the hood, what kind of tires I had, or how many miles were on it when I first got it. But I can tell you about the tape deck.

Cassettes. Tapes. Looking at a cassette now, the first thing that comes to mind is...really? Cassettes were the worst, *the absolute fucking worst* way to listen to music. The sound was terrible, they weren't built to last...and yet, they were the only way to make mixes for your friends.

Or in my case, to listen to in my car.

When I was in high school, I'd run upstairs after dinner and hole up in my room for hours. My room was like the Batcave—blinds drawn, maybe one lamp on in the corner. And I'd perch myself in front of my Panasonic tape deck, grabbing records and CDs off the shelf, sequencing the tapes I'd need for the various travels I'd be making in the Monte Carlo.

At this point, it bears mentioning that I was a total music nerd in high school ... but not in the same way that indie kids are today, with their ironic appreciation for classic rock. When I was in high school, we had respect for rock's forefathers. AC/DC wasn't AC/DC, they were AC/*Fucking*/DC. Rush? Well, Rush was quite simply the most excellent and technically proficient three piece band in the history of rock and roll. And while I'm on this tangent: Fuck you, indie kids.

Back to the car: before I turned the keys in the ignition, I'd reach into the glove box, where I had a stack of Maxell tapes waiting, each one with its own distinct purpose.

If I was driving to see the grandparents, for whatever reason, I would play a tape of '70s art-rock songs. Maybe something from the Peter Gabriel era of Genesis, like "Colony of Slippermen," or some shit like that. Or David Bowie...Oh. My. God. David Bowie. The *Diamond Dogs* album—that three-song sequence, the troika, of "Sweet Thing/Candidate/Sweet Thing (Reprise)." Amazing. And to spice things up, I might toss in a song by U.K. Anyone remember U.K.? They had an electric fiddle; that's all you need to know.

If I was cruising around with my dumb buddies, we went LOUD. Iron Maiden, the *Number of the Beast, Piece of Mind*--songs like "Run to the Hills," "The Trooper," "Die With Your Boots On." Maiden, Priest, Sabbath--*Those* were the albums to blast as we drove up and down the mean streets of Skokie. Or at least Main Street in Skokie. Between Crawford and Skokie Boulevard. Then back to Crawford, and back again to Skokie Boulevard.

If I had to drive anywhere with my parents, I'd play to my audience. "Hey, dad, it sure is cool to be driving you around for once. Wanna listen to some music?" At that point, I'd whip out what I thought was the perfect mix of

Rolling Stones songs. I'd start with "Jigsaw Puzzle," jump from there to "She's A Rainbow," then slam into "Live With Me." Then, I'd pull it back to the modern day, something from the *Tattoo You* album. Can't go wrong with Keith Richards and "Little T&A."

Understand…the tape deck was freedom. By extension, the car was freedom. When I was driving the Monte Carlo, it meant that I was in charge. It was my show to run. I was the ruler of my automotive kingdom.

Now when I was going to pick up a girl, or group of girls, which was … what's the right word? … *rare,* I had to be ready with the right songs. My friends relied on songs from Roxy Music's *Avalon* album to set the mood. Cool album, for sure. I love "the Main Thing," for instance, and Bryan Ferry's the Sean Connery of rock and roll, but I just didn't want to be that obvious.

I would put together a tape with Bryan Ferry, but something like "Is Your Love Strong Enough." That was a B-side, a soundtrack song from the movie *Legend.* If you wanted it, you had to buy it on twelve inch from the Record City on Oakton Street.

In hindsight, perhaps one of the reasons girls weren't frequent guests in my car is that my idea of cool was a song from a Tom Cruise movie about unicorns and fairy princesses which also starred that fucking dwarf Billy Barty.

Let's fast forward to today. When I leave here tonight, I'm going to get into my beat-to-shit '98 Toyota Corolla. I couldn't tell you how many miles are on the car, but I know there are a lot. I couldn't tell you what kind of tires are on the car, even though I bought new ones at Firestone two months ago.

I do know, however, how I'll be listening to music in the car. I'm going to take my iPod and plug it into my iTrip. Then I'm going to jack the iTrip into the cigarette adaptor under the stereo. And I'll turn the stereo to 106.9, which is how I receive the iTrip's signal. And because I'm in the moment, I'll have the iPod set to "Is Your Love Strong Enough" by Bryan Ferry.

Thanks for coming tonight.

And within seconds of walking off the stage, the house band of Steve Frisbie, Liam Davis, and Gerald Dowd jumped on stage to play "Is Your Love Strong Enough."

My "First Time" experience was incredible; truly a wonderful way to usher in 2011.

Early in the 1990s, 80s nostalgia was a big deal. For a while at least, it was fun to make references to breakdancing, Thundercats, and the Rubik's Cube.

At the turn of the century, entertainment media rushed to capitalize early on the impending waves of 90s nostalgia. Contrary to the previous decade, the rush to rekindle 90s memories felt premature:

(Saturday, July 17, 2004)

<u>90s Nostalgia</u>

I watched "I Love the 90's" off and on this week on VH1. As the series of shows edged closer to the end of the decade, it was truly difficult to feel any sense of nostalgia. Last night, the usual roster of talking heads dissected the events of 1999, and all I could think was, "wait a minute, this shit JUST HAPPENED." The memory lane trip just seemed too premature. Let Fred Durst completely slide into has-been obscurity before dragging him out as a hilarious example of bad 90's taste.

Does fan enthusiasm drive band reunions, or does the "glory day" nostalgia of individual band members drive them to have reunions?

Whichever the case, unless we're talking about the Smiths, every band that's ever broken up seems to get back together eventually.

On that note: Hey, Morrissey and Marr, we're not getting any younger here. I'd like to see "What Difference Does It Make?" in concert before I die.

(May 13, 2010)

<u>Band reunions</u>

Bands that achieve some level of success, be it having a hit song, critical acclaim, or a devoted fanbase, never need to stay broken up forever. If timed well enough, a band can tour themselves into a retirement home.

Open any British music magazine and comb through the concert listings. The first thing you'll realize is that bands long forgotten—many assumed to be broken up years ago-- are still actively touring.

The secret to a successful band reunion? The band has to stay broken up for a long time.

Nostalgia's a powerful thing. As we age, we tend to retreat to the comforts of our young and dumb days, those days when music hit us hard and left a mark. For some, those comforts can be relived by seeing Psychedelic Furs at Metro next month, or Soundgarden at Lollapalooza ... maybe even Rush at the Charter One in July (Time Machine tour! Time Machine tour!).

The most successful and enduring reunions are those where a band waits a decade or more to resurface. That allows enough time for the band's legend and meaning to truly sink in. More importantly, it opens the door for the following generation to discover the band and grow up wishing that they'd had the chance to see the band in the first place.

Plenty of bands do the reunion thing right. Soundgarden's return is well-timed. Alice in Chains pulled off 2009's comeback of the year. Neither band was in a hurry to reunite, for very different reasons. In both cases, the reunions happened at times that felt appropriate.

That's where Billy Corgan messed up. Smashing Pumpkins called it quits in 2000. Less than five years later, Corgan used the local press to herald the band's return (and by band, I mean Corgan, Jimmy Chamberlin ... and others). The Pumpkins were never gone long enough to let the wave of nostalgia wash them into the future. This once-mighty and influential band is currently struggling to remain vital with its new music, while those who grew up with them in the 90s have moved on. Give it ten years, Billy. They'll be back.

And then there's Limp Bizkit. Sweet Christ, and then there's Limp Bizkit. Whatever the acceptable "stay broken up time frame" is for bands, Limp Bizkit needed to add five years to that number. I have no doubt that there will come a day when Limp Bizkit's special brand of once-lucrative mook rock will again strike the right chords with the public. When it does happen, though, it'll be borne of the same sense of ironic appreciation that allowed '70s disco nights to happen in bars and clubs in the early '90s. Dear Fred Durst, it's too soon.

When I wrote that piece about band reunions in 2010, I wasn't aware that the topic was one that had bugged me for years.

I'd completely forgotten that I wrote this, five years prior:

(June 13, 2005)

<u>"Goodbye" doesn't necessarily mean "forever" in rock</u>

Every band reunites. Seemingly, there's no cause or dollar amount incapable of reuniting fragile artists who've spent years embroiled in acrimony.

The latest reunion? Pink Floyd. While there's something to be said for seeing Waters and Gilmour on stage again, the thrill of seeing these post-50-year-old guys belt out stoner anthems from the 70's seems kinda, I dunno, sad.

Along those lines, it feels somehow wrong to go see the Stones this time around. Charlie should be at home in bed, not touring the world and performing "Heartbreaker" for the eight millionth time. By not attending, I'm sending a message; a message to the band to stay put and enjoy their senior years.

To repeat: no band stays broken up forever. Though it took 13 years for them to get there, grunge titans Soundgarden finally reunited in 2010.

(January 28, 2010)

<u>Soundgarden Reunion</u>

On New Year's Eve, Chris Cornell announced via Twitter, "The 12 year break is over & school is back in session. Sign up now. Knights of the Soundtable ride again!" Like Billy Corgan before him, a failed solo album paved the way for a much more-welcomed band reunion.

So, yes, Soundgarden is returning after almost 13 years. When they left us, they were touring behind *Down on the Upside*, a fairly standard album that garnered merely average reviews. Back then, in the few years post-*Superunknown*, it felt like the band had run out of steam. And that proved to be true.

At its best, Soundgarden is an ambitious, tough-as-nails, band fronted by one of the best voices in rock. In a live setting, on a good night, the band could transform weaker album tracks into absolute epics. And this is the band I hope we're going to get.

The first big piece of rock news this year is certainly exciting. Is it too early to speculate on a Lollapalooza headline slot?

It wasn't. They were one of Lollapalooza 2010's big acts, along with Green Day and Lady Gaga.

Sometimes, nostalgia can be fueled by hindsight. That's the type of vision that brought me to the point of appreciating Stone Temple Pilots.

(December 7, 2004)

<u>My Stone Temple Pilots Epiphany</u>

Around the time of the last Velvet Revolver show, I remember reading a review in one of the dailies that said Stone Temple Pilots keep looking better in hindsight. I couldn't agree more.

When (debut album) *Core* came out, STP was derided, blasted, and mocked by critics and music snobs everywhere. The band's timing didn't help, coming out directly after Nirvana and Pearl Jam had already staked their respective territories.

I wrote the band off along with the critics, assuming that Stone Temple Pilots was just another major-label constructed flash in the pan. Even so, there were moments I appreciated (e.g. "Crackerman" off the debut, the riff on "Interstate Love Song," and the dense, pummeling guitars on "Sex Type Thing").

STP's third album, *Tiny Music*, caught my ear initially because it was clearly different from the first two. Though the Beatle-like melodies and added layer of experimentation hooked me for a moment, I still had myself convinced that I shouldn't listen to them recreationally.

When *No. 4* came out in 1999, I saw the band play at the House of Blues in Las Vegas. It was one of the most eye-opening shows I'd ever seen: small room, big sound, and a frontman with an undeniable, larger-than-life presence. Something totally clicked over for me that night. The STP catalog suddenly made sense. The songs weren't clichés or Pearl Jam hand-me-downs; they were actually *good*. I couldn't believe what I was thinking. After years of being a passenger on the refuse-to-take-STP-seriously bandwagon, there I was in Vegas, singing a wholly different tune.

Like the review said: In hindsight, they keep sounding better and better.

Throughout junior high and high school, I had my ears glued to Chicago rock radio. Powerhouse stations like WMET, the LOOP, WCKG, and WXRT introduced my friends and I to the quote-unquote classics: AC/DC, Black Sabbath, and Jimi Hendrix.

In high school, it was important to have a favorite band, an artist who you knew everything about and owned everything by. Led Zeppelin was my pick.

John Bonham was long dead by the time I was able to go to concerts, leaving me to fantasize for years about what seeing a Zeppelin show was like. Watching the disappointing and tedious concert film The Song Remains the Same *didn't properly convey the feeling.*

Although I dutifully bought every Robert Plant solo album from Pictures at Eleven *on, I never saw him perform live until 2005.*

(July 12 2005)

<u>Robert Plant at the Auditorium</u>

Robert Plant totally exceeded my expectations on Saturday night.

His face is lined with age and years of hard living, but when I closed my eyes on Saturday, I heard the youthful and spirited golden god whose voice carried me through my early teen years. Hearing a pure-sounding Plant in the acoustically-perfect Auditorium Theater was as close to rock nirvana (Manic Nirvana?) as it gets.

Helping Plant hit all the right notes was his gifted backing band of much-younger players; their palpable hunger and energy seem to keep the Plant watered and growing.

The show's setlist was something of an oddity. Plant played a heaping amount of new songs, one cover from the last solo album, and a generous batch of Zep songs.

Not that the set list was bad, necessarily, it was just ... missing a lot.

For a guy who's now cataloged two decades worth of solo material, I found it odd that he didn't touch any of it. I wouldn't have minded a "Heaven Knows" or "Pledge Pin" dropped in between "That's the Way" and "Black Dog."

Speaking of the Zeppelin songs, "When the Levee Breaks" was definitely the standout moment of the show. "Goin' down to Chicago ..."

Nostalgia doesn't get any more depressing than watching an aging metal band slowly morph into a real-life Spinal Tap.

(October 25, 2009)

<u>ANVIL</u>

The Metallica documentary *Some Kind of Monster* told the compelling story of the most successful metal band *ever* as it faced almost-certain self-destruction. By the movie's midpoint, you stopped rooting for the guys (at least James and Lars) and started wishing that they'd fall off the cliff they were stampeding towards.

The opposite of that (and non-fiction equal to *This is Spinal Tap*), *Anvil! The Story of Anvil*, has you begging by the movie's midpoint for someone--anyone--to *just give the band a fucking break already*. Just one break. One.

The core story is about Anvil as the archetypal metal also-ran; a band that influenced bands like Metallica, Slayer, and Anthrax, but met with none of the same acclaim or financial reward. Early in the movie, we see frontman Steve "Lips" Kudlow, in his 50s, delivering food for a public school catering company. In his spare time, he remains focused on Anvil, taking any gig or opportunity that presents itself; usually to humiliating conclusion.

The secondary story, probably the more enduring one, is that of friendship and love. Unconditionally encouraging and supporting Lips through the lean years (decades) are family--wife, child, and siblings--and his best friend and Anvil drummer Robb Reiner. The relationship with Reiner is the backbone of the film, and it's a relationship that runs thicker than blood. They fight like siblings, trust like spouses, and joke like roommates.

By definition, "Anvil!" is a rock doc. In reality, it's a character-driven film, played out with honor, emotion, and honesty by Lips and Reiner. Their tenacity and resilience to keep the band moving forward, despite the fact that Anvil's shelf life has long since expired, is both heartbreaking and inspirational. I pulled out my digital copy of *Hard 'N' Heavy* after finishing the movie tonight. I feel like I owe the band at least that much.

There was a lot of buzz behind the movie early this year, some of which has returned with the DVD release. Netflix it. Buy it. Do something. The band's not getting any younger.

YAMMER OF THE GODS: INTERVIEWS

CHAPTER TWO

There was a time in my career when I thought I'd have the resources and energy to transcribe every artist interview I'd ever conducted. Silly me.

Here are a few I took the time to turn into text several years ago.

(August 11, 2003)

<u>A Perfect Circle</u>

Metro-last night. A Perfect Circle returned to Chicago as part of their club tour to set up their forthcoming sophomore CD, *Thirteenth Step*. As of 6:30, the line to get in to Metro went down Clark to Grace, wrapped around Racine, and went back down Waveland. The band went on just before 9:30, and left after a tight, focused set, mainly pulling songs from *Mer De Noms*. Earlier in the day, I sat down with drummer Josh Freese and new touring member James Iha.

JVO: I get the impression that, with this band, it's kind of Billy (Howerdel)'s sandbox, and people are invited to play in it.

JF: Yeah, but this time, I jumped in, and pushed him out of it.

JI: He kicked his ass.

JF: Kicked his ass in the playground. Yeah, you know, the first record, he had everything pretty much written. Most of the first record is just Billy, myself, and Maynard (James Keenan) and Paz (Lenchantin) played a little bit on it, and Troy played on one song, but it was basically everything that Billy had already pretty much mapped out in his own head about how he wanted it to go. Most of it was already recorded, like on his Pro Tools home studio rig, and I just basically came in and did drums on top of it, and Maynard sang over the top of it. This time, it was more of a band effort, and more of a collaborative thing between Billy and I, and Billy and Maynard, and the three of us, and Geordie,

our new bass player, came in towards the end of it, and
played some bass on some of it.

JVO: How happy is he, by the way, to reclaim his real name?
(Geordie was Twiggy Ramirez in Marilyn Manson's band)

JF: I think he's happy. Sometimes, you know, I can tell ...

JI: It's kinda like small talk though, now. It's just like, "hey,
you changed your name ..."

JF: Yeah, I think sometimes, it depends on his mood.
Sometimes he's happy that it's back to Geordie, and the
other times, if he wants to be like, there's one of those few
times you want to be recognized, or want to be introduced
to somebody, and they'll be like, "This is Geordie." And the
person's like, "Who?", and they turn around and walk away.
But he might think if they think it's the other guy, they
might go, "Oh!" They don't make the connection sometimes,
you know.

JVO: Since the world hasn't heard the new album yet,
contrast it with Mer De Noms.

JF: I think it's better. The first record we made seemed a little
harsh and a little, like, just big wall of guitars the whole
time. This record, I think, breathes a lot more and I think it's
a little bit more organic sounding than the first record. It's

not as processed, it doesn't sound like it's gone through so many different channels and modes of electronic outboard gear and crap.

JVO: You guys caused some trouble with the Offspring recently, right? What was that all about?

JF: That was kind of an inside joke. The Offspring guys are old friends of mine from Orange County. Actually, I played drums on their record that's not yet out.

JVO: Of course you did. It would be easier having a conversation with you, Josh, discussing the bands whose albums you haven't played on.

JF: Yeah, exactly. The Outfield ...

JI: Cutting Crew ...

JVO: You played on Avril Lavigne's album.

JF: Shhhhhhhhh.

JVO: But you still rock, of course ...

JF: I like her, she's nice. Never met her. (pause) Oh, yeah, the Offspring, yeah yeah yeah, 'cause I worked with Guns N Roses, and they were working on this record that's still not out, it's tentatively titled *Chinese Democracy*. Then, when I was in the studio with the Offspring, those guys thought it would be funny if ... they decided, "We're gonna name our album *Chinese Democracy*". They didn't, but they sent out a press release, because legally you can. But, I told them, if they tried, Axl, I'm sure would try to make their lives hell however he could. So, they went ahead with telling everyone they were going to do that, and Maynard wanted to up the ante once by contacting the Offspring, or having me tell the Offspring that we were going to put on our website that we're in litigation with them. (It would've read like) we're suing them over the title, even though you can't sue anybody, and Axl would be at home going, "Why's A Perfect Circle and the Offspring arguing over that title? That's my title! They can't be fighting over that title!" But, neither of us ended up calling our album that, so ...

JVO: Maynard is an interesting guy. What's he like? Our vision of Maynard James Keenan, from the outside, is he's kinda nutty.

JF: He is kinda nutty. I think he's kinda nutty, but he's kind of un-nutty, too.

JI: This sounds like old-school Hollywood. Like, "He's a nut, isn't he?"

JF: (laughing) Yeah, he's a real nut ...

II: Did you see him last night? He was a nut last night. He went off, and he was just crazy.

IF: He's nutty, and sometimes he's un-nutty.

IVO: I phrased the question poorly. It was a more delicate way of saying, "So, guys, seriously, that Maynard's out of his fucking mind, right?"

IF: A lot of people think that Maynard's out there, and in a way, when it comes to doing what he does, I think you do have to be a little bit out there to pull it off or be as convincing, because he is serious about it. He's not messing around, he's not contrived when he's singing or doing what he's doing. He can tap into some nuttiness (laughter). On the other hand, he's a guy that, amongst his friends and his circle of people he feels comfortable with, that he loves, whether it be family or friends, he can be very normal, and very generous, and very fun, and funny, just a regular guy. But, then, there's the other side of him, which is the "unregular" guy.

II: The other night, he told me, "Look at your guitar rig when you go up there, onstage. He had taken a picture of the two guys from Air Supply ...

IF: He put them behind my drums, too! Maybe it was different nights, but ...

JI: Yeah, he put it on my pedalboard. I was like, "what, what??" And I was like, "oh, oh, okay ..."

JVO: James, the last time we saw you on stage as a part of a band ...

JI: Yes.

JVO: It was the Smashing Pumpkins.

JI: That is correct.

JVO: I've always had the impression of you as someone who was okay being behind the scenes, and keeping a low profile. You've kept a low profile since the Pumpkins break up. What dragged you back in? What made you say, "I want to go on tour again"? I'm sure it's a pretty grueling proposition.

JI: Yeah. I definitely needed a break from being in a big rock band. I just wanted to not have the pressure and the whole thing of being a big alternative rock band. I was saying to somebody, the only way I could be persuaded to go back into a big band is if it's a great band, and these guys needed a guitar player, and they're all really great guys, and I like what they do. That's about it.

IVO: And there are lots of personnel threads you can draw back and forth between the A Perfect Circle and Smashing Pumpkins family trees. I also think, thematically, Smashing Pumpkins had some dark moments ...

JI: They both were and are dynamic bands. They both have the lightness and the darkness, and ...

JF: The nuttiness.

JI: The music's great, so ... It was a challenge to me, but it was also exciting.

IVO: Do you plan to stay on?

JF: Do you want to say it in front of me? I can leave the room if you want.

JI: I only joined, like, three and a half weeks ago, so it's kind of premature.

IVO: Would you like to?

JI: Um, you know, this is the band, for all crazy, nutty purposes ...

JF: It all came about pretty quick, in the eleventh hour. Geordie's only been working with us since January or

February. And, you know, James just about a month ago, it's like it all ... I was stressing out more about finding a guitar player than those guys were. It was like two months ago, and I was like, "we're on the road in eight weeks!"

JI: I know! I was like, "why did they wait?"

JF: Billy was like, "Oh, we're cool. We'll find somebody. Maybe so and so ..." And I'm like, no I think it's going to be a lot harder than you think. And then, it got down to the wire, and it was just like perfect timing. Billy emailed you or something, James?

JI: Yeah. I was in Sweden, hanging out with this band on our label.

JVO: The Sounds?

JI: Yeah, and I get this email from Billy, who's like, "Hey, do you want to go on tour for a year, and play with A Perfect Circle?"

JF: At first, you said you couldn't do it, right?

JI: Yeah, but it happened.

JVO: Alright, we're out of time. Quick fanboy comments ... Josh, remember "Clowns Are Experts"? That was awesome.

JF: That's a great song.

JVO: James, remember the video for "Tonight, Tonight"? That was cool.

JF: I like that you know "Clowns Are Experts".

JI: I don't even know that song.

JF: It's an old Vandals song. We never play that song. People request that song when we're playing live, and we've all gotta divert our eyes. Actually, I don't mind, I like that song, but a couple of the other guys in the band try to forget that it was ever written.

(January 12, 2005)

Scott Ian of Anthrax

As both a constant talking head fixture on VH1's "I Love the…" shows, and comic book/graphic novel fan, it's easy to sometimes forget that Scott Ian is an icon…an honest-to-God, metal icon. A giant, really. I called him on his cell as he was winding his way through a blizzard somewhere in the Colorado mountains.

JVO: Next month at the Aragon, it's the benefit for the Dimebag Darrel Memorial Fund. It's you guys, Disturbed, SoiL, and Drowning Pool. Let's flash back to 1992. Just two years after *Cowboys From Hell* came out, Pantera hit with *Vulgar Display of Power*. Meanwhile, you guys were already at the top of the metal heap. Belladona was out, Bush was in. You guys were ruling the world, just as Pantera was starting to seriously turn heads. Did Anthrax feel the impact of Pantera as it was happening?

SI: Yeah. Even way before that, even before Philip was in the band, we always knew what a powerful band they were. Once Phil joined, it kinda gave them, I think, that's when they really focused on what they were going to become. When the "Vulgar" record came out, well even before, *Cowboys From Hell* really was the record that put them on the map. And then "Vulgar" was the one that really solidified it. It's just a classic. So, yeah, we always kinda knew, we saw it very early on, just what a great band they were. And there was the one piece that was missing, then they filled that spot, and nothing was going to stop them from that point.

IVO: What was your relationship with Dimebag? I know he had nicknames for you-"Baldini," "The Jew." He's played on Anthrax songs…

SI: He played on the last three Anthrax records. We were friends for a long time. We'd known each other since 1986. Especially for guys in bands, I know every guy in every band, but there's very few I can actually say I was friends with more than just "Hey, what's up?" He was one of the few guys that I kept in touch with, and was more than passing acquaintance.

IVO: The news of the shooting was catastrophic. How will this affect live shows? Will it affect Anthrax?

SI: I don't know. I don't know. It's not going to change the way we approach what we do, I can tell you that much. I would assume that places that didn't have barricades before, will now have barricades. Look, it just makes sense. Even before something insane as this happens, barricades just make sense anyway, just because, from an insurance point of view, everybody wants to stage dive and have fun, and do things like that, but then they turn around and sue the band when they break their arm or something. That's kinda frustrating. We've been pretty much playing only shows with barricades for a long time, anyway.

JVO: I know everyone's doing at least one Pantera cover for the show next month. What are you guys doing?

SI: We know a bunch of songs already anyway, so it's not hard for us to pull one out.

JVO: This is going to be a very cool show, from top to bottom, just one borne of awful circumstance.

SI: It sucks that this show's even happening, truthfully. That weekend after Dime was killed, I was watching that concert for George Harrison on television, just wondering how come nobody ever does something like this in metal? If anyone deserves it, it certainly is Dimebag. When I was in Texas at the funeral, I saw David from Disturbed there. I said, "Hey, man, I was watching this thing…" He's like, "Dude, I'm already on it. I've already got places on hold, and blah-blah-blah." I was like, it's just good to know that people were thinking about trying to do something to help people out.

JVO: Thinking of how Chicago regards you, we know that you're a New York guy, but we would like to co-opt you as one of our own.

SI: Well, you've got Charlie there now, so...

IVO: I suspect part of the reason you're still a New Yorker is that you need to be close to the VH1 studios at all times.

SI: (laughs) I don't need to do that.

IVO: You've become the voice of pop culture disgust for metal fans everywhere.

SI: Yeah, really.

IVO: The time between the last two albums, *Volume 8* and *We've Come For You All* seemed very long. This time, it seems like you're throwing your fans more bones. There was the live CD/DVD recorded here, and you just put out *The Greater Of Two Evils*.

SI: Right.

IVO: Does redoing the old songs invalidate the originals in any way?

SI: No. I don't know what other people think, but not to us. No, not at all. We've been playing these songs live forever, most of 'em anyway, with John singing them. We weren't looking to remake the songs, we weren't going in and redoing these things as studio versions. We just recorded them live in the studio, basically, as if you'd come to see us tonight. That's how we would've played those songs. The whole record was for the fans, basically. They voted on it on the website, and we gave them what they wanted.

JVO: You gave them what they wanted, and they gave you tattoo pictures in return (there's a mosaic of fan tattoos in the jewel case album art).

SI: Exactly. (laughs)

JVO: Around the time of *We've Come For You All*, you had said that "Safe Home" was probably the best Anthrax song ever written. Are you writing now for a new album; and, if so, how do you best that?

SI: Good question. We haven't gotten together yet. The plan is to get started pretty soon here. The holidays are done now, it's gonna give us some time to focus on where we're gonna go on this next record, so…

We've got a bunch of things in the works right now. Charlie's just trying to get his act together, you know, he just moved out there to Chicago. He's getting a studio together there. As soon as we're able to, we'll start jamming. I know he's been writing riffs, and I know I've got ideas, and Rob's got ideas… It's just a case of us getting together and seeing where it goes. I am excited about it. The eighteen months we spent touring for *We've Come For You All* have really given me a great state of mind, going into the next record.

__IVO__: I saw you twice on that tour. Last time, was at Oasis 160, which closed down not all that long after you played there. Coincidence?

__SI__: (laughs)

__IVO__: There in the crowd that night, was comic book art deity Alex Ross. What a night, Anthrax and Alex Ross. Big geekfest for me (Wilmette comic artist Alex Ross did the art for *We've Come For You All* and *Music Of Mass Destruction* for Anthrax, as well as countless industry-leading works for both D.C. and Marvel Comics).

__SI__: Right.

__IVO__: Are you looking forward to any of the comic movies coming up-*Elektra, Constantine, Sin City, Fantastic Four, Batman Begins...*?

__SI__: I'm definitely looking forward to *Sin City*. I think *Constantine* should be okay, too. That looks all right. *Elektra*? No, not at all. Sadly, most of the Marvel movies, outside of X-*Men*, most of the Marvel movies are pretty terrible, in my opinion.

JVO: Even *Spider-Man 2*?

SI: Yeah, you know, I'm not a big fan of the Spider-Man movies. I like the first half of the first one, when he's discovering his powers and whatnot, and then I thought the Green Goblin was terrible. I like parts of *Spider-Man 2*, but overall, I don't know, not so into it. It's just too big and commercial for me, truthfully.

JVO: One tier below that, then, would be *V for Vendetta*, with Natalie Portman...

SI: I didn't even know that was being made.

JVO: The guys who did the Matrix are doing it.

SI: They're doing V? Didn't know that. Cool, well, if anyone can do a good job with a comic movie, it should be them.

JVO: Well, Scott, thanks for the time. See you at the Aragon next month.

SI: All right, see ya.

(May 1, 2002)

<u>Black Rebel Motorcycle Club (Peter Hayes, Nick Jago, Rob Turner)</u>

<u>James VanOsdol</u>: You were in town last night opening for Spiritualized, which was your last gig with them. Now you're going off to Europe?

<u>Nick Jago</u>: Yes...playing, hopefully.

<u>JVO</u>: And they love you out in Europe, they loved you even before this album came out.

<u>NJ</u>: Ahh, a little bit.

<u>JVO</u>: Well, the BBC did.

<u>NJ</u>: Yeah, yeah. No they did, they got behind it pretty early with "Whatever Happened to My Rock N' Roll."

<u>JVO</u>: And this album has been out for over a year now, although new people are still discovering this album. Is it still a good representation of who you are at this stage in time?

<u>NJ</u>: Yes, well it's close. Close enough yeah. Yeah, it's changing a bit, but it's close enough. The songs are strong enough to make up for whatever...the change.

JVO: Are you writing while you're on the road?

NJ: A little bit, yeah. I mean we don't have a whole lot of time. The nice thing is that before we kinda left we've got a ton of half songs and stuff.

JVO: Works in progress?

NJ: Just keep those in mind, yeah you know. There's a ton of that kind of thing, you know. Yeah you just try to finish them.

JVO: It seems to me that BRMC has a very clear vision of who you are and who you want to be. Has the vision been consistent from day one or has it evolved?

NJ: I dunno. We've got a vision of it, but I don't know if that's coming across all the time, because you're having to deal with this filter and that filter and then you know, one person to the next person. Words get jumbled and pictures get blurry, but you know it's just the fun of it at the same time. I don't really expect that our story has been told, I don't really think that everyone, you know, has us all summed up yet, so it kind of makes it worthwhile at the same time. You think about that a lot. Why say anything anymore, we've done a ton of interviews. Why even say anything if people've got us all summed up, then that's it.

IVO: It does seem like you're holding stuff back...not right now necessarily, but in general.

Peter Hayes: I don't know where to start.

NJ: I don't know how you sum up anything, I mean we're twenty-some years old. What the hell do we have to sum up? We're just a bunch of kids messing around, there's nothing to sum up at all.

IVO: Well the music has landed you in a very enviable position. People do love and admire this record, I count myself as one of them. Your record company has basically allowed you to do your own thing, which is fairly unheard of and kind of scandalous in a way. You have to be pretty satisfied with what's going on.

NJ: Scandalous is the key word.

PH: It's a good word.

IVO: You can count as admirers people who I'm sure you personally love, whether it's a Johnny Marr or a Jim Reid-that's the Mary Chain reference I'll make today. Is it cool to get the validation from your pop heroes or is it cooler to get the validation from the masses?

NJ: They are both good, I think. It's a really nice thing, I mean Johnny Marr or whatever, you know the guys from Oasis or something like that. You know, it's kind of a wow. That's nice that they give us a nod. That's it. It's just really nice, but it doesn't make them any more. Them giving us a nod is no more than anyone else giving us a nod of appreciation. Not really, I mean honestly, but you know it's nice.

PH: It's just encouragement, it gives you a little bit more encouragement.

NJ: In the big scheme of things.

JVO: Let's talk about "Red Eyes and Tears". Bitter song on the record, what's the story behind that?

NJ: Bitter?

JVO: I've got to think that somewhere along the lines there was a broken relationship that was beyond repair.

PH: They're all broken beyond repair.

JVO: Well, "Love Burns" is an optimistic song, in a sense.

NJ: They are all optimistic, you know. There's always a glimpse of light somewhere buried beneath the darkness.

PH: "Red Eyes" is similar to that, too. The words kind of twist around and are not there where you can take it. You know. Either way, really. It plays around in there where it's kind of like because I'm not crying anymore. It can be happy, that's all I'm saying.

IVO: It's all a matter of perspective. Walk me through the songwriting process. I'm sure that a lot of the songs that made it to the album were a long time in the making. The first album is the one that takes forever to finally get out. After that, you kind of find your rhythm. When you guys attack a song, how does that work? Does one of you come up with a lyric and then you all jump on it or does the music come first?

NJ: We've gone every which way so far. It started with acoustics for the most part, and then there are a couple we just left behind because the song(s) wouldn't work live; (they) belong on the back porch and should stay there. And you know there's the "up till 7 AM trying to just writing a song while you're recording," don't know where it's going to lead. The best, my personal favorite, is just live, just playing out. Don't know where it's going, but we're listening to each other and you start screaming out words on top of whatever is out there. And that's just the most natural way to me. "Awake" came out that way and "Punk Song" came out that way. This new song we've got is kind of like that. It's kind of the wave of the future. The better we get, the more we can do that. It's hard to say right now because we are kind of in between our old writing style and our new one.

JVO: You mentioned "Punk Song," a song that addresses a lot of what's going on in mainstream music. It seems that BRMC is in the right place at the right time. Do you feel like your timing is pretty on?

NJ: I don't know. I don't know if it really has anything to do with us.

(September 24, 2004)
<u>Josey Scott of Saliva</u>

<u>JVO</u>: Just before *Survival of the Sickest* came out, you promised that it would be a six-pack of American whoop-ass. What about your fans that'd hoped for a keg?

<u>JS</u>: (Laughs)

<u>JVO</u>: The first three songs off the disc: "Rock and Roll Revolution," "Bait and Switch," "One Night Only," are, by and large, about the trappings of fame and success. That's kind of a tricky thing to write about, and for people to relate to. I'm assuming you were in an interesting spot when you were writing these songs.

<u>JS</u> : Yeah, I think that this is a personal record, but I think it's a relatable record. I'm… talkin' about the trappings of fame and success, but I'm talkin' about 'em (with) a point of view…from where I came from. (A) blue collar point of view…a southern boy that came from nothin' and doesn't even have a high school diploma's point of view. You know, growin' up poor, not knowing where my next meal was coming from, like the rest of the guys in the band. …And then getting a little taste of this and that, and what you do next is more of what the record is about…being hurled into the vortex of not being able to attract flies to shit and then havin' it all. I think that's relatable. I think that people will

somehow identify with that. I think the whole thing is a life lesson, because I'm not saying, "Hey I'm all right, look at me." I'm at the dance, and it's not about the dance. It's about your friends and your family, and people that love you, and the people that care about you. It's not about cars and houses and pussy and stuff like that.

JVO: Although all of the above are fantastic.

JS: (Laughs) Although all of the above are fantastic, I agree.

JVO: You wrote about 20 songs for the disc. Where did the ones that didn't make it end up? Will we see them eventually?

JS: Yeah. They'll be in movie soundtracks and video games, stuff like that. We really hate it when we don't get to use all songs, 'cause they're like your little kids, you know. You want all of 'em to make the cut; but, unfortunately, there's only so much room on a record, so you use the rest of 'em for other opportunities.

JVO: "Click, Click, Boom" almost didn't end up on *Every Six Seconds*; that was a last-minute thing. Were there any similar experiences with *Survival...*?

JS: That's a good question. I think on that record and during that time period, we had a little taste of, a little bit of, success and we had to go hog wild. I call it, being friends with Nikki Sixx, we had to act like Motley Crue for a while. We had to do all the drugs, and be with all the girls, and drink all the alcohol, and just see how far our human bodies could go. You know, how long we could teeter on the edge before we fell off. I think on this record we learned from that experience. I think we took more time to get in the back of the bus with an acoustic guitar and an old Wal-Mart tape recorder and really beat this album out, and we were prepared when we walked in the studio. We were ready.

<u>JVO</u>: I like "Razors Edge", which is good old-fashioned, southern-fried, rock and roll. You've got Brad from 3 Doors Down on it. Where did that song come from?

<u>JS</u>: I was in a really bad relationship for a long time, one of those relationships that you kinda just get stuck in and you're not really in love, but you're not strong enough to let go. There's a song called "Open Eyes," its kind of a ballad. It's about me finally having the strength to let that relationship go, and cut it loose, and there's another song that expresses the anger that I felt from that relationship, it's called "Carry On" and then there's "Razor's Edge." (It's) more about me finding somebody else. Really finding the someone that was meant for me and falling in love again, and I say that I will hold on to forever, then walk right through this open door. I think that's what I've done.

IVO: You've been through a lot recently. You stopped taking drugs. You got married in Graceland earlier this year. How often does the past of Saliva, the "Motley Crue" Saliva, collide with the current model of Josey Scott?

JS: Every once in awhile, you gotta let your hair down and show your ass, I guess. I think we've tamed that beast. I think we've learned enough lessons from that, and we've realized that we don't have to act like Nikki Sixx all the time...just some of the time.

IVO: I know you used to hang out with Dimebag Darryl (Pantera, Damage Plan), and if you're hanging out with Dimebag Darryl, that means there are a lot of strip clubs involved. Still true?

JS: That is absolutely true. We were just discussing that the other day (laughs). We were talking about, come over to Saliva's bus and we're watchin' movies and laughin' and getting ready to go on stage or...or hanging out. And you will have Damage Plan or whatever, parked behind us, and they'll be falling out of the bus, breaking Jack Daniel's bottles, trashing guitars...you'd think that they'd probably do that in front of fans, or they would do that on stage, but their doin' that backstage where there's nobody lookin' (laughs). You know, they're just stumbling off their own bus, trashing their own guitars, breaking their own whiskey bottles for each other's entertainment. Its true rock and roll indulgence. It's fun to watch, and fun to be a part of.

IVO: I'm getting the image of you guys watching movies on the bus, and maybe sharing some popcorn.

JS: That's a lovely image. (laughs)

IVO - It's a folksy image, but you look at Saliva and you think "Man...here's a band I never want to get into a bar fight with." In truth, you guys are just a bunch of southern gentlemen, yes?

JS: Yeah, absolutely. We've always prided ourselves in being southern gentlemen. We've always prided ourselves in extending a hand and a smile. When I got signed, my mother told me, "Son, there's enough assholes in the world to go around. You don't have to be one." And so I pride myself in always being a gentleman. I've always been nice to fans, I've always signed autographs, and been a sweetheart. But we will, when our kindness is taken for weakness, whoop your ass. Ain't no doubt about it. It's just the way it goes, I guess. When your kindness is met with somebody who's a dick, I guess you have to retaliate.

IVO: Tell me about some of your other interests. I know that you have an interest in acting.

JS: mmmmhhmmmm ...

JVO: How far do you want to take that?

JS: I really love acting. I'm going to take it as far as far as I can. I think it's an extension on my creativity. It keeps me busy, and I do a lot of painting, as well. I write a lot of poetry. I try to keep my creative juices flowing. I think, like Elvis Presley said one time, "It's not from me, it's through me. I just have the best seat in the house."

JS: I gotta quit collecting cars, I know that.

JVO: Since you grew up poor, was that one of your big indulgences when you did start making some money?

JS: Oh, cars? Definitely.

JVO: If we were to pull into your warehouse, or garage space, what would be that one car that would just make our jaws drop?

JS: Probably Elvis' '69 Cadillac limousine. The one that would probably make your jaw drop right away is probably the Smokey and the Bandit Edition '79 Trans-Am, (that's) pretty hot. It's just like the one the Bandit drove in the movies, so ...

JVO: A lot of bands that broke around the same time as Saliva aren't necessarily still around, and they're not really thriving in the same way that Saliva is. You've had the luxury to build an estimable catalog. What's the secret to your endurance?

JS: I think it's honesty, and integrity to our writing. I think that we honestly tried to keep it interesting, to bring our fans what they enjoy most from us, but to throw 'em a curve ball, you know to continue to throw a creative curve ball. To not write the same hit songs over and over and over again. With *Every Six Seconds*, it was Hip-Hop influenced, because that's where we're from. *Back In Your System* had a little alternative influence, cause that's where we're from. And now, we're in (the) era of *Survival of the Sickest*, and it's, like I said, (a) true straight-up, six-pack of American whoop ass, and that's where we're from. They all have the common denominator of honestly being a part of us, but we try to keep it interesting, we try to keep it fresh and we try to continue to raise the bar and we try to continue to be creative and push ourselves to the next level.

JVO: What do you think of when you think of Chicago?

JS: I've always loved Chicago. I've played there ever since they had the Thirsty Whale!

JVO: Yeah!

JS: I don't know if anyone remembers that, back in the old late '80's when we used to come up there, we were in another band called Blackbone. We used to come up and play the Avalon Club, Thirsty Whale, The Vic Theater. We got a little bit of history in Chicago. It's only 6 or 7 hours from Memphis depending on how fast you're driving, so we definitely jetted up there and spent some time.

JVO: Now that we know how long it takes you to get here, no excuses. We want to see you here more often.

JS: (laughs) No doubt, brother. And when we come see you live, we're gonna bring the kegs, baby.

In 2005, principal Motley Crue songwriter Nikki Sixx was trying to get his band Brides of Destruction off the ground. Joining him in the band were L.A. Guns guitarist Traci Guns, drummer Scott Coogan, and singer London Le Grand.

Seeing as I can fondly remember buying my vinyl copy of Shout at the Devil *from Record City in Skokie the year it came out, talking to Nikki was a childhood goal realized.*

(2005)

<u>Nikki Sixx</u>

<u>JVO</u>: It's got to be daunting to start a band from scratch, having done what you've already done with Motley Crue.

<u>NS</u>: It's actually the opposite. It's invigorating because we set out to do this band on the premise that it was going to be fun, we're going to make the music that we wanted to make. We didn't really care if it came out or didn't come out. By doing that, we kind of set ourselves up for success. We funded everything ourselves, we rehearsed, and when we wouldn't rehearse, we hung out. We got to know each other as a band, kinda became a gang. And then, other people started reacting to the music, without us getting into the whole "sales pitch" thing, on how come we're a great band and all this stuff. People were reacting to that, and record companies were reacting to that, and we were like, "Well, that's unexpected."

JVO: Isn't the album essentially a demo that got dressed up?

NS: Aren't all the greatest first albums demos? It's very important to us. We've got 50 songs now, for the next record.

JVO: I'm glad you brought that up. There's that concern that, if Motley Crue heads out on the farewell tour, Brides of Destruction will be put on the backburner and never heard from again.

NS: No. If anything, this is my main band. When Motley's over, this will be my Motley Crue.

JVO: Is it hard, or even necessary, to distance yourself from Motley Crue with this band?

NS: No, it's a completely different kind of band. I'm proud of (Motley Crue), proud of what we've done musically. Very few bands get to put out a "Greatest Hits." I put that thing on the other day, and I was like, "we really did some good stuff together, didn't we?" It's fun to be able to stand there and go, "You know what? We sold over 40 million records, man. We toured the world many, many times. We shook things up, we did it on our own terms." (I) love the guys in the band, (but) probably this band, if there's ever a band, this band was not built to last. The fact that we lasted even to a second record has always amazed me. And I think with the pinnacle being Paramount Pictures signing the band for a movie deal based on our book (*The Dirt*), and I think where we all said, "You know what, let's end on an up note. Let's not just drag it out."

IVO: You've described the movie adaptation of *The Dirt* as a "story of survival," more so than a story about Motley Crue.

NS: I believe so. I believe it would be very narcissistic and egotistical of us to make it really about us. It should be more, and will be more, about when the person's watching the movie, they go, "Yeah, I've been through that. God, how did those guys survive that?" It's more about that, instead of (being about) Vince Neil and Nikki Sixx. That's so limiting.

IVO: What's most amazing about *The Dirt* is the fact that you remembered as much detail as you did.

NS: (laughs) It took all four of us, but we did it.

IVO: You hit the top, and it seems like you weren't ready to handle it.

NS: You know, I don't know if anybody ever really is. It's just bizarre, one day you're some kid, and the next day, you're on your own jet with a waitress with her top off, giving you lines of cocaine, and calling you "Mr. Sixx," asking if there's anything else you need. You know what that means ... And you think "Wow, this is pretty cool. It seems like just the other day, I was listening to Deep Purple *Burn* in my friend's car and thinking, "how do people do that?"

JVO: *The Heroin Diaries* are coming out in October ...

NS: We're talking about them coming out now next year, because I'm so focused on the Brides and everything.

JVO: And this (*The Heroin Diaries*) is Nikki Sixx at his darkest moment?

NS: I would say so.

JVO: Is it therapeutic to relive this stuff?

NS: It's therapeutic. I've never been shy about revealing my demons to people. It is a bit therapeutic, and maybe it's helpful.

JVO: Other people have said that, once you're a recovering heroin addict, even though you're not using, you think about it every day. Is that the case with you?

NS: Not in my case. I don't think about heroin anymore. It's something that was a huge nightmare in my life.

IVO: Here in Chicago, we've never had a scene as hedonistic and decadent as Motley Crue-era Los Angeles, but is there stuff here that appeals to you?

NS: Chicago is an amazing city. We always have great shows there, great fanbase. I've never had a bad experience there.

IVO: Do you have any favorite Chicago stories, personal or sleazy?

NS: Oh, there're a few decadent things that've happened in Old Chicago ... we'll leave that for the next book!

CHICAGO MUSIC and *CHICAGO ROCKED*

CHAPTER THREE

Of everything I've accomplished professionally, my greatest point of pride is the effort I've thrown behind promoting and supporting Chicago music. As host of "Local 101" on Q101 (WKQX-FM) and "The Local Zone" on The Zone (WZZN-FM), I had the great pleasure of hearing local music first and then having the opportunity to break it on the air.

"The Local Music Showcase" (later "Local 101") was my first on-air gig, the result of a well-received "demo tape" I mocked up for Q101's then-Program Director, Bill Gamble.

The mock-up show included me doing song intros and outros, as well as clips from interviews I recorded with local artists exclusively for the demo. The three artists interviewed were Nubile Thangs (an unknown band to this day, but I enjoyed them), Loud Lucy (more on them later), and the man-mountain, schizophrenic, omnipresent scenester, Wesley Wills.

As far as I was concerned, "Local 101" was the best gig in town. It didn't pay "Eddie and Jobo" (B96/WBBM-FM) money or have the prestige (or sense of elitism) of a WXRT airshift, but for me, it was the right show in the right place at the exact right time.

I was Q101's Chicago music voice and advocate until I left the station in December, 2000 (To confuse the issue, I returned to Q101 six years later, was fired 1 ½ years after that, and returned two years after I was fired. Radio, everybody!).

Throughout my career, I met and worked with hundreds of people far more talented and interesting than myself. Two of the nicest guys I ever met were Matthew Leone and his twin, Nathan.

Matthew made headlines in 2010 for jumping into the middle of a domestic abuse situation that was unfolding right in front of him.

As he walked out of his Near West Side apartment, he heard a woman scream. It wasn't the type of scream people think to make; it was one of primal terror.

Across the street, he allegedly saw a woman being violently beaten by her husband. Without thinking, he knocked the husband off his spouse. Matthew managed to log a 911 call in before the alleged assailant, a much larger man, attacked him.

Matthew was semi-conscious when the ambulance took him to the hospital. He lapsed into a coma not long after that.

His efforts made him a hero, and that heroism almost cost him his life.

(July 24, 2010)

<u>Matthew Leone</u>

I waited a while to write this. By now, the savage beating that Matt Leone endured has been well-documented and discussed. Since then, some really decent people have raised their hands to help. It's been an interesting lesson in the depths and heights humanity can hit, all in the same context.

I started communicating with Matt and his twin Nathan at the tail end of the 1990s, when I hosted Q101's "Local 101" program. At the time, the Leones were working to get their band, the Blank Theory, off the ground. The songs on the first two Blank Theory albums were smart, chunky, rock slammers that flew in the face of the "cookie monster" sounds that had become cliché by 2000. The band reeked of potential, and around the turn of the century/millennium, I fully expected them to follow in the same trajectory as Chevelle, whose beginnings and shows in Chicago often overlapped with the Blank Theory.

In person, the Leones always came across as decent, likable, and hard-working. Described another way: Archetypal Midwesterners. When I hosted my final "Local 101" show in December, 2000, they were on a short list of people who stopped by to be part of it. They weren't there to promote their band; they just wanted to be supportive. Over the following years, my interactions with the Leones became infrequent, due to my own shifting jobs and responsibilities up and down Chicago's FM dial. We'd periodically trade emails, and even managed to hang out once or twice in the past five years (which is more my issue than theirs; I don't get out much). The twins are simply two of the nicest guys I've ever worked with in "the scene."

When I heard about the incident that put Matthew in the hospital, it knocked me into a funk. He's too decent, too good-hearted; and in this case, too much of a hero, to be in this terrible circumstance.

By inserting himself into that awful domestic abuse scene, he did something I know for a fact I wouldn't have had the balls to do—he tried to help someone in peril without considering the risk to himself. And let's be clear: Matthew's not a big guy. Both the twins look like they could use more butter, burgers, and ice cream in their diets. And yet, despite his size, Matthew behaved heroically in an every-second-counts scenario. Justifiably, his actions and their results have resonated across countries and social circles.

I donated some of my personal possessions to the Through the Pain auction: a Josh Freese-autographed A Perfect Circle platinum *Mer de Noms* record and a Matt and Lars-autographed 10" vinyl edition of Rancid's *Let's Go* album. Since then, artists like Metallica and Madonna have kicked in items for the auction. It's been remarkable to see the global response to Matthew's plight.

The local response has been nothing short of incredible, too. I'm really proud of Q101 for hosting a 16 hour Request-a-thon for Matthew. I'm also floored that Billy Corgan and Metro pulled together a benefit for Tuesday, using a ticket raffle as a really clever way to fundraise.

I left Nathan a voice mail a week or so after everything happened, not expecting a response. I can't even imagine the volume of concerned email and voice mail messages he's had to sift through, to say nothing of the touch-and-go status of his twin and the endless press inquiries he has to field. And yet, Nathan called me back. That's the kind of guy he is. And for that matter, that's the kind of guy his brother is, too.

I had lunch with Matthew in April, 2011. I spent most of the meal fighting back tears as he shared his experiences with me.

As I mentioned, the brutal attack put him in a coma. A few weeks after he came out of the coma, a mostly routine follow-up surgery broke bad and led to him flatlining on the table.

Coma? Flatlining? No other way to say it -- Matthew Leone is lucky to be alive.

As Matthew recalled—with astonishing lucidity-- the events leading up to his beating and the dark days that followed, he relayed the details with warmth and unnecessary humility. He's an exceptional human being, and I'm a better person for knowing him.

His alleged assailant made bail and continues to walk among us. I sincerely hope that justice catches up to that monster.

Because of my experience in hosting local music-focused radio shows, I occasionally get asked for advice. I'm not very good at telling artists what to do, but I'm excellent at telling them what not to do:

(January 26, 2010)

How not to build a band

As I've mentioned overandoverandover again, Facebook's not for me. I still doggedly believe that it'll go the route of MySpace within three years or less. Furthermore, I can't understand why people focus so much energy building out personal content on a website that's not their own. I'll occasionally post status updates on my page, though they're usually just of the "announcement" vein, and they're directly copied from what I'm posting on Twitter.

But I digress...

I have a few hundred "friends" on Facebook, some of whom I even know. I got a Facebook message today from someone who noted that I have a lot of "friends" on the social net site. He then asked me for a favor: he wanted me to recommend his band's fan page to all my Facebook friends in order to impress a record label.

Two things about that:

1. I've never blindly recommended that all my friends join a fan page, nor have I ever endorsed a band in that way.

2. This is a fundamental problem with baby bands and the music industry: the belief that amassing passive names is the right way to build a career.

If labels are still impressed by--let alone considering artists on the basis of--empty numbers, then they rightfully deserve to continue circling the drain.

Bands: make good music. Build a fan base of truly interested, passionate people who want to interact with you online and see you on stage. It's not about tonnage, it's about superserving that core group of followers. Reinforce their belief in you, and their enthusiasm will be shared and spread with others.

Careers aren't made by record companies (I can point to plenty of examples to the contrary), and they're certainly not made because a bunch of sheep click "Join" on a fan page.

Before publishing this book, I threw a few years of my life into a book about Chicago music in the 1990's (working title: Chicago Rocked*).*

The 90s were an extraordinary time for music and music events in Chicago. Once the decade ended, I was driven to capture the memories and emotions of the time in print.

As of 2005, I had a book deal in place. In 2007, the publisher and I parted ways. Then, in 2009, I launched a desperate campaign to self-publish Chicago Rocked, *using crowdfunding site Kickstarter.com to raise money. The good people at* Gaper's Block *were nice enough to let me use their website to state my case:*

(August 27, 2009)

CHICAGO ROCKED: CHICAGO MUSIC IN THE 1990s

"New York and L.A. are like the girls you want to fuck; Chicago's like the one you want to marry"
  – Mat Devine, Kill Hannah

So much for spoilers. That quote is the final thought of my book, *Chicago Rocked*. I suppose I'm not really spoiling too much; the book technically doesn't exist yet, and there's a chance it might stay that way. More on that in a bit.

Whenever I followed a trail of empty PBR cans to Wicker Park for a local band's set in the '90s, I thought, "Someone really should write a book about this era of Chicago music. Someone should commit the stories of these amazing bands to print. Hey, wait, that someone should be me."

Why the '90s? For one, the decade fostered a sense around town that anything ... anything ... could happen. How else to explain the Casio-wielding, schizophrenic, headbutting man-hulk Wesley Willis getting a record deal? Material Issue frontman Jim Ellison getting urinated on in public? Ministry's Al Jourgensen recreating Sodom and Gomorrah in a recording studio?

After playing the part of "second city" stepchild for so long, Chicago suddenly mattered to the rest of the world. Dozens of bands were courted by ponytailed major label weasels. Dozens more bands gave major labels the finger, continuing to create challenging sounds for their own art's sake (thanks, Tortoise; thanks, Steve Albini).

During the '90s, I hosted a Chicago music radio show ("The Local Music Showcase," later "Local 101") on Q101 (WKQX).

Running the show was like being given an "All Access" pass to the scene — and I didn't have to blow anyone to get it. I did have to suck up to my Program Director at the time, but it's not like I felt dirty afterward.

Through the show, I got to know all the noisemakers around town; if not personally, then through their recorded music or live performances. The show gave me a foundation for the book, but the idea of actually writing it seemed fairly overwhelming. Before I totally committed myself, I solicited some band friends for feedback. "You're insane," one said. "Can you make me more famous in your version of the story?" asked another. Chicagoans have a knack for self-deprecation.

I started working on the book (then given the working title of Chicago Rocked) in 2005, around the same time that I was let go from radio station "The Zone" (WZZN). Perfect timing--I was suddenly free to fill my days with interviews for the book. I sat down with Steve Albini at Electrical Audio. I hung out with Ed Roeser (Urge Overkill) at the Andersonville Starbucks. I met Josh Caterer (Smoking Popes) for pizza in Des Plaines. I recorded dozens of phone interviews, transcribing everything as I went.

Envisioned as an "oral history," Chicago Rocked was originally scheduled for publication by a regional press. My relationship with the publisher ended in 2007, and I then made the decision to put the book on a shelf.

And there it stayed.

I'd spent too much time ... too much energy ... and in the end, I had nothing to show for it. I was disgusted with myself and needed a break. "It's not you," I told my book, "it's me."

When I finally opened the manuscript back up, I had a minor revelation. My "oral history" method was fucked. I needed to rewrite everything, starting from the very beginning. So, one night, in the middle of the winter, I did just that. Two rewrites later, I was confident. Excited. Rocking.

If I learned one lesson from the musicians I interviewed and wrote about, it's that "D.I.Y." is the way to go. I couldn't let my enthusiasm for this book go through the soul-sucking process of searching out a literary agent. I couldn't spend years schlepping the manuscript to publishers who are losing money faster than they can pay it out. I had to take matters into my own hands.

I'd heard stories of musicians like Josh Freese and Jill Sobule turning to their fans to help fund their projects. Fans pledged contributions for projects based on specific financial tiers, each of which brought different rewards from the artist (a liner note mention or a song written about a generous benefactor, for example). Web 2.0 glossaries call the concept "crowdfunding." The word "fun" is right there in the middle of it. Count me in.

I decided to use Kickstarter.com, a website designed to help artists bankroll projects through tiered crowdfunding support. Once I got approval from the site to use it for Chicago Rocked fundraising, I panicked. "Oh shit," I thought, "I'm really going through with this. What kind of money do I actually need to make this happen?"

I considered everything, including offset printing, copy editing, indexing, mailings, legal support, ISBN, and design work. My estimate came in at a jaw-dropping $17K. The thought of asking for that kind of coin made me uncomfortable. And then I told my inner self to suck it the fuck up and start chasing down the money. Shilling for cash is a necessary evil; this book needs to be read. I worked the pledge tiers so that most everyone who kicked in would be included in the finished work. And then I took the Kickstarter page live.

All Kickstarter projects have a 90-day limit for pledges. Chicago Rocked fundraising officially began on June 17, and concludes on September 16. As I write this (8/24/09), I'm 30% to goal, with 70 backers committed to $5,086 of the full $17,000. If the goal isn't hit, nothing gets collected and the book doesn't get published.

If Wesley Willis (bless his batshit-crazy soul) were alive today, he'd wrap this up by saying "Rock over London, Rock on Chicago ... United, Fly the Friendly Skies." Then he'd give me a headbutt and make me shout "RAH!"

I'm simply saying "Chicago Rocked, pledge money."

Now c'mere and give me a headbutt.

Remarkably, I managed to generate over 10K in pledges for my book. Sadly, it wasn't enough. After licking my wounds for a year, I decided to take an honest inventory of what went wrong with my Kickstarter campaign.

(October 23, 2010)

Kickstarter Success Story

Last year I tried, and failed, to fund a book project of mine using Kickstarter. I don't regret the 90-day experience, but I have learned a lot since then.

Last week, my friend Patrick launched his own Kickstarter project to build out and complete a comic book art gallery (brilliantly called "The Rogues Gallery").

Patrick reached his funding amount only 12 short hours into the campaign.

The simple reason for the project's success is that it's a great idea which appeals to a talented and passionate community of artists and fans. Beyond that, Patrick asked for a relatively modest amount, making the funding all but guaranteed.

Simply put, Patrick had the right idea, he understood his audience, and he didn't ask more of his audience than they were willing to give.

When I plotted out what I actually needed to take my Kickstarter book project to completion, I accounted for a lot of big ticket expenses. Among them:

Professional manuscript editing

Page layout and cover design

Offset print run of 1500-3000 copies

Fair and respectful payments for the three principal photographers who contributed images to the book

Professional indexing

Legal representation

Web hosting to support the online home of the book

Those (and other) expenses had me estimating my needs at a shocking 17K. I knew it was a ballsy amount to pitch, so I worked my ass off to raise awareness and generate interest over those three months. Along those lines, I:

Did interviews with any media outlet that would have me (Good morning, Rockford!).

Wrote a new blog entry every day about a topic specific to the book for the full 90 days of fundraising,

Called and contacted old friends, new friends, and people I barely knew, trying to spark interest up and down every possible online and offline social network.

In the end, I hit $10,294. It was a massive amount, for sure; just not massive enough. At the end of the 90 days, the funding board was wiped clean and I had no finished book to show for it. I had asked for too much money to fund a fairly niche book ... in a recession. My book strategy of "doing it right" led me to not doing it at all.

If I were to use Kickstarter again, I'd use it to launch a project that required significantly less funding, or I'd at least find a way to better handle costs.

From a "sizzle" perspective, I'd also take the time to record a video message for my funding page, rather than rely on a static picture of, say, Al Jourgensen.

Back to Patrick and The Rogues Gallery, funding's already gone $1300 over the target. In one short week of activity, Patrick has taught me how to do this right. I'm not ready to test the Chicago Rocked waters again, but there will be other projects down the road ...

I suppose this book qualifies as one of those "other projects."
Thanks again for buying it.

From the unpublished Chicago Rocked, *an excerpt from my Introduction:*

Before the national proliferation of Chicago artists, there was the grunge explosion in Seattle that shot out Nirvana, Pearl Jam, and Soundgarden. At that point, only a small handful of Chicago acts--Michael McDermott, Material Issue, and Eleventh Dream Day among them--had major label deals.

Once the Seattle scene began to wane, the music industry had to have another "it" city. And wouldn't you know it? Chicago got tagged.

1993 was the Year of Our Lord for the Holy Trinity of Chicago rock: Smashing Pumpkins, Liz Phair, and Urge Overkill. The Pumpkins' second album, *Siamese Dream*, instantly became one of the albums that helped write the charter of the fledgling "alternative nation." Liz Phair's ballsy debut, *Exile in Guyville*, was so good it put rock critics in the awkward position of trying to find more synonyms for "seminal" (to which I humbly suggest "cum splashy"). Urge Overkill's major label debut for Geffen, *Saturation*, while never financially matching the hype it created, was one of the most consistent and exciting rock albums released that year. Just ask Urge Overkill.

The successes of those three acts drove record companies insane with desire to stake their claim on Chicago's quote-unquote burgeoning scene.

Steve Albini, the sage-like voice of reason for the independent community, famously warned against the evils of major labels in his 1993 Baffler article, "The Problem With Music."Leading with, "Whenever I talk to a band who are about to sign with a major label, I always end up thinking of them in a particular context. I imagine a trench, about four feet wide and five feet deep, maybe sixty yards long, filled with runny, decaying shit."

Albini went on to articulately and mathematically spell out how stacked the system was against bands in the major label puppy mill. Did anyone listen? Some did. The Jesus Lizard did for a few years, at least.

But, man, it sure was easy to dismiss Albini as an indie elitist. After all, unsigned bands were routinely filling clubs like Metro and Lounge Ax. "Alternative" bands like the Red Hot Chili Peppers and Nine Inch Nails had become popular culture's ruling class. Those factors combined made it seem possible for a band to crawl out of the garage one week and, with the right buzz or muscle behind it, become an in-demand, thisclose to inking a deal, "next big thing" the following week. It felt exciting. Hell, it was exciting. Albini be damned.

Sigh. So many bands in Chicago inked deals. The list was huge and genre-spanning, from Certain Distant Suns to Triple Fast Action, Smoking Popes to Pulsars. The city's scenesters and tastemakers (I might've been one for a minute or two, prior to a move to suburbia and the acquisition of a Costco card) were sure that at least a handful of those bands would step up and carry the already-lit Pumpkins/Liz/Urge torch. And none did (note that Wilco and Disturbed blew up on a massive scale after the 21st century had begun, to say nothing of what that Kanye guy did for hip-hop after the turn of the century).

The letdowns came fast and furious. Without exception, every near-success to come from Chicago was taken down or out by bad financial deals, industry politics, drug addiction, alcohol abuse, hubris, or ordinary, everyday bickering. In essence, stupidity both external and internal. The implosions came so frequently that I began to suspect our city's music scene was cursed. No one could catch a break. Somewhere on the North Side, the Chicago Cubs shook their heads empathetically. Somewhere just a mile or so southwest of there, Steve Albini shook his head knowingly.

As I was trying to get Chicago Rocked *crowdfunded in 2009, I supplemented my efforts with a daily blog-within-a-blog called "90s in 90 Days." I took the opportunity to focus on one aspect of the Chicago scene in the 90s every day, sometimes using deleted scraps from my manuscript, other times telling stories that didn't really fit in with the overall narrative.*

(June 1, 2009)

<u>It's Over</u>

The curse of hosting a local music show--or any radio specialty show, for that matter--is that Program Directors hate the idea of it. Specialty shows are programmed by the on-air host, and the music that's played on them is mostly unfamiliar. Worse, in the mid-90s (and probably through today), the Sunday 11 p.m. time slot was a ratings dead zone, when most current-based music stations couldn't scare up a listener to save their souls.

The Local Music Showcase was cancelled twice, ratings cited as the reason in both cases. I'll always remember the first time the axe fell. I made a habit of pretaping band performances for the show during normal weekday business hours, when I had the benefit of a sound engineer on site. On the morning I'd booked a noisy little band called Lorax to come in for a recording session, I got pulled into the Program Director's office.

Once I sat down, the P.D. told me politely and professionally that the local show's ratings were dragging the weekend ratings down, and that it was being pulled off the schedule immediately. It had nothing to do with me, I was told, it was just business. The whole conversation took five, maybe 10, minutes.

I walked out of the office and looked at my watch. The band was supposed to arrive in minutes ... I had to tell them to turn around. Suddenly, I heard my name paged on the intercom: the band was waiting for me in the loading dock.

I'm sure the band members ditched out of work to come down to the studio. They were probably looking forward to the added exposure, too. After shaking their hands, I said awkwardly, "Um, the show's just been cancelled. We can't do the recording."

After that morning, I fell out of contact with the band. They probably hated me (consider the messenger killed), but I was also too embarrassed by the situation to go chasing after them once the show was revived.

From where I was sitting, Chicago music in the 90s wasn't defined by obvious names like Liz Phair, Steve Albini, or Billy Corgan.

Wesley Willis more accurately illustrated how quirky and blissfully unconventional the scene was, and reinforced the general sense that anything was possible in it.

Chicago's music scene (mostly) threw their arms around Wesley, a diagnosed schizophrenic who was haunted by voices, visions, and profound emotional trauma. Wesley was a fixture around town, seen nightly at places like Metro and Empty Bottle, camped out in a corner, listening to music in his headphones while cranking out eerily accurate Chicago cityscapes on posterboard.

He was a musician, too. He had recorded … 40? 50?... self-produced CDs of music that all followed the same warped composition road map.

The "music," such as it was, was built on a preprogrammed loop run through a Technics keyboard, which Wesley would speed up or slow down, depending on his artistic needs.

His lyrics were most frequently about bands or people he knew (there was a "James VanOsdol" song on his Drag Disharmony Hell Ride *CD). Other common subjects included uncommon acts of animal cruelty ("Suck a Cheetah's Dick") and infamous newsmakers ("Richard Speck," "Saddam Hussein").*

Each song ended with a marketing catch phrase, the Wesley Willis equivalent of Porky Pig saying "That's All, Folks!" You knew that the "harmony joyride" was near its end when Wesley barked something along the lines of. "Sony. It's a Sony," or, "United. Fly the Friendly Skies."

His saga as a Chicago artist was fascinating to follow, and I sometimes intersected with it.

(July 25, 2009)

<u>"Wanna buy my CD?" -Wesley Willis memories</u>

Schizophrenic. Dangerous to himself. Friend to artists. Inker of Chicago skylines. Wesley Willis was the "Where's Waldo" of the 90's scene, visible wherever live music happened--from Lounge Ax to Empty Bottle, Thurston's over to Metro.

One of my most lasting memories of Wesley came from WKQX/Q101s "Twisted 2" concert at the Rosemont Horizon (now Allstate Arena). I was working part-time on the air; hosting "The Local Music Showcase" on Sunday nights, and pulling occasional fill-in shifts on the weekend. We must've been short-staffed that year, because my then-Program Director, Bill Gamble, asked me to do a stage announcement that night. I got slotted to introduce the show's second band, Goo Goo Dolls.

The idea of walking out on stage at the Horizon, as a complete unknown on the Q101 airstaff, didn't so much scare me as it did unnerve me. I decided that I wanted to do something memorable. Scratch that--I needed to do something memorable. I asked Wesley Willis to come to the show and do the stage announcement with me.

Wesley Willis was ... a handful. He was an unpredictable, driven-by-demons, giant of a man with a scar tissue patchwork forehead. The concert promoters were concerned about keeping him reined in back stage. Q101 management was concerned about keeping the concert promoters from flipping out. I was concerned about not shitting myself the second my stage mic went live. Long story short, the stage announcement was fine. It confused about 85% of the crowd and annoyed another 10%. But, man, that 5% really got a kick out of it.

But that's not my lasting Wesley memory ...

Wesley always had his D.I.Y., casio-driven, CDs on hand, hustling them to anyone who ended up in his line of vision. Walking around backstage at Twisted, he found a potential buyer: Perry Farrell (Jane's Addiction, then of Porno for Pyros). "Wanna buy my CD?" Wesley asked Perry, who at the time was traversing a cosmic plane different from the one you and I share. "It is a rock and roll record that will take you on a harmony joy ride." Perry smiled enthusiastically, then said in that fey, Crispin Glover, voice of his, "Sure, man, cool." Seconds later, one of the alternative nation's pied pipers was fishing for a ten-spot to trade for a Wesley Willis CD. Unforgettable.

Another memory from the same show comes from Stoley, who co-hosted mornings on Q101 for a while and also fronted the Lupins, "Wesley Willis was in the Goo Goo Dolls' dressing room, and Johnny Reznik finds a large white envelope on a table in their dressing room. He says, 'What is this?' And he opens it up, and he pulls all of these papers out of it, and he goes, 'This looks like a record contract. This is a record contract with Def American.' And he starts leafing through it, and he goes, 'Who's Wesley Willis?' I'm like, oh, Wesley left his record deal in the Goo Goo Dolls' dressing room. I'm like, hey, I'll get it to him. So I took it and found him, and I'm like, Wesley, don't leave this lying around."

A great deal of attention was given to those Chicago bands who managed to net fat record contracts in the 90s. For every one of those success stories, there were 75 more bands left to struggle on the local scene. One of my favorite forever-obscure bands from that period was BOOM hANK.

(July 1, 2009)

BOOM hANK plays to the South Side

BOOM hANK's 1995 release on Pravda, *Nuisance*, was rootsy, but with an edge to it that only a calloused heart could create or appreciate. Think Counting Crows if they drank PBR while shooting pool to Husker Du records. Listening back to *Nuisance* in the present day, I'm as surprised now as I was then that the band never got enough attention to even be considered obscure.

Singer Stump Mahoney remembers the difficulties of being a band that played originals on the south side, "We could certainly play clubs on the south side, but it was frustrating. We would play this one place called Riley's Daughter and we do a handful of originals, and mix them in with some cover tunes, but the covers were always Pravda label artists, or some other bands that were either signed to larger independents or even major labels: we'd do Souled American songs, Replacements tunes, Pixies ... After playing some of these places, the management would say, 'Hey, nobody knows your music. You've gotta play stuff that they know.' And we'd say, okay, and the next time we'd come by we'd announce, 'Okay, this is a John Cougar Mellencamp B-side,' and we'd go into a Replacements tune or something. And that eventually just wore on us."

As a music fan, I've always preferred seeing a band on the rise, rather than at (or post) its commercial peak. Chicago is the type of city that offers those opportunities on a nightly basis.

(June 15, 2009)

The thrill of discovery

I vividly remember seeing the New Rob Robbies at the Empty Bottle in 1995. Don't worry if you don't recognize the band name--their obscurity is kind of the point here.

I'd decided to see them play live after receiving a 12" EP for "Local Music Showcase" consideration. They were good back then, a proverbial "diamond in the rough." In fact, one of the guitar riffs on the EP--chunky, angular, and awesome--has stayed with me through today (though admittedly I couldn't tell you the name of the song it's from).

The night they played the Bottle, I got there early and grabbed the best seat in the house, towards the eastern most wall in the back of the club, directly facing the stage.

Turns out, getting there early wasn't really necessary. I was one of maybe 15 people in the room, a figure that aggressively included the bar staff. I remember the band apologizing for the turnout. It didn't bug me at all.

Waiting for the band to take the stage, I was reminded of one of the true pleasures of being a music fan: the thrill of discovery.

In these post-web 2.0 days of hyper-advanced social networking and niche marketing, our opinions are largely shaped and informed by digital peers. And while getting "turned on" to new music by a digital pal is swell and all, there's nothing like that feeling of being there first. It's this exact sensation that drives overprotective fans to scream bloody murder when their little secrets become the talk on everyone else's lips.

Sitting there at the Empty Bottle that night, rocking solo to the New Rob Robbies, I felt empowered. The band was good, not great ... but it didn't matter. I was in the moment, savoring the thrill of discovery.

Ever have one of those moments where you say the absolute worst possible thing at the most unexpected time?

One of my most memorable embarrassing moments happened at a hometown gig for Certain Distant Suns.

(June 7, 2009)

My Hootie and the Blowfish Moment

I was at Dome Room late one mid-90s weeknight to see Certain Distant Suns.

I wandered the venue once I got there, looking for a familiar face to talk to. Within minutes, I ran into the local promotions rep for the band's label, Giant. She was there with her boyfriend, Soni (pronounced "Sunny"), and after introductions, we made industry small talk. I'd just started doing a few "regular" (non-local music based) airshifts on Q101, and she asked how it was going.

"Great," I said. "Even though I have to play shitty bands like Hootie and the Blowfish, I love it."

She looked at me with a nervous smile. "Soni plays drums for Hootie and the Blowfish."

I can't remember my reaction. I remember it feeling something like an "out of body" experience. The shame haunts me to this day.

Lesson: there's no need for snark when in the company of strangers.

From the early, "oral history," manuscript version of Chicago Rocked *comes this Loud Lucy outtake which always makes me snicker. Maybe it's just me.*

In the mid-90s, Loud Lucy got to travel the country in support of their Geffen album *Breathe*. Their touring van wasn't quite the urban assault roadster most bands envision when they first dream of going on tour. Drummer Mark Doyle and singer/guitarist Christian Lane explained:

Mark Doyle: (The person who gave us a van) was a friend of Christian's family. He had a flower shop in LaSalle, Illinois, or wherever that small town is they're from. He gave him the van to use for touring.

Christian Lane: It was little black van, but it had little white flowers and white letters, and it said "Jerry's Flower Barn" on it. It was such a little sissy van—Jerry's Flower Barn.

MD: This was our first trip to New York; (we've) never been to New York before. We had a map, but it wasn't a street map—it was a map of the country. We went across the Washington Bridge and I saw 1st Avenue. I'm like, "Oh, perfect. Take a right here. 1st Avenue, we'll just go down until we hit 10th Street, and (then) we're done." Well, 1st Avenue obviously runs the length of Manhattan. So it's like saying "Take a right on the Kennedy Expressway." We had no idea, so we started driving.

All of a sudden, we noticed we were driving through Harlem. We heard gunshots, and everyone was shitting in their pants. Everyone that could be was hunkered down and hiding. I was just thinking, "This is bad, this is bad. We're not going to make it, this is bad." We finally found (our destination), and got out of the van. Everyone was still pretty scared. And on the side of the van was spray-painted "THE NIGS."

We got tagged somewhere while driving in Harlem. Must've been at a stop sign or something. Somebody just ran up to the van and spray-painted the side of it. So on front of the van, it's got this little flower sign in all this (feminine) type of writing, and on the side we had "THE NIGS."

CL: Mark said, "Jerry's Flower Barn. If you're the Nigs, and you saw Jerry's Flower Barn, why would you be offended? Why would you be threatened by Jerry's Flower Barn?" That was Loud Lucy for you.

Blake Smith, songwriter/vocalist/guitarist for the band Fig Dish, is one of the most articulate and funny guys I've met in Chicago music. In this interview excerpt, he talked about a big "buzz show" Fig Dish was scheduled to play in the early 90s.

"We thought it'd be pretty fun—it was us, Hush Drops, Triplefast (Action), and Nectarine. We decided that every band would do one side of *Hot August Nights*, the double-live Neil Diamond record. We did it in August at (music club)Avalon.

"Our rider was just a keg of beer and ten pizzas; it was just a show for fun. But then word got out that these four bands who'd all been getting scouted by labels were playing. All of a sudden, Capitol shows up…Geffen shows up.

"Before the show, Wes from Triplefastaction said, 'I'm sorry to be a pussy, but we're going to play a Triplefastaction set. We want to get a record deal. We can't do this in front of all these label people.' John from the Hush Drops said, 'Yeah, we're going to do a Hush Drops set.' Nectarine said, 'We're going to do a Nectarine set.' Fig Dish, on the other hand, we gave them Side Three of *Hot August Nights*. I'll never forget, the guy from Geffen walked up to me and said, 'Well, you fucking blew that one. Have fun in Chicago for the rest of your life.'"

An especially moving live performance I remember seeing in the 90s was a Stabbing Westward set that only a handful of others got to witness. Q101 used to routinely host "Live 101" sessions, live "mini-concerts" performed for invited guests inside a local recording studio (most frequently the Chicago Recording Company in Streeterville).

Stabbing Westward did a Live 101 session just as both the band and lead singer Christopher Hall's personal life were disintegrating. As Christopher explained to me:

"One of the last shows we played in Chicago, we ended up playing at the Riviera; it was when we played with Placebo and Flick. I had to go to court in the morning, (take care of my) divorce, and then go to Q101 to do an acoustic set of these really dark, my marriage is falling apart, songs from *Darkest Days*—that's what the whole album is basically about. I had to try and sing, after actually seeing the culmination of this album.

"And the reality of…'Holy shit, I just ended my marriage today, and here I am singing these songs acoustic. That was really weird. When we did the show that night, I was a mess. I think I ended up drinking a bunch of Jagermeister before to get through it."

Growing up in the 80s, the two Chicago artists I was most familiar with were Naked Raygun and Ministry.

Raygun was the "cop coat" band; the local punks with the "whoa whoa" vocals and the buzzcuts. Their music, tough and melodic, inspired later-day Chicago artists like Smoking Popes and Rise Against.

Ministry was the "ohmygodfuckingscary" group. In the late 80s, Ministry mastermind Al Jourgensen turned his back on the dance sounds that defined the band, and repositioned Ministry as an industrial-metal hybrid (a move that was then totally groundbreaking).

Ministry's music was an audio syringe loaded with sex, drugs, violence, humor and rage. The live shows were martial and primal.

Consistent with the band's musical output, Al Jourgensen's private life became a portrait of extreme hedonism. As Ministry's star rose, so did Jourgensen's status around town. His around-the-clock bacchanals were emblematic of the "rock and roll lifestyle," and legendary in their own time.

It cannot be overstated: Al Jourgensen lived hard and partied harder. From Chicago Rocked*:*

"I had a circle of hangers-on," Jourgensen said. "Basically, Smart Bar would close at 4, and they'd start lining up at 4:30 to get into the studio.

"The newest engineers had to be doormen. It was like Studio 54: Either you had liquor, drugs, money, or women. (And if you did), you were *maybe* allowed to come in. They'd stand out there for hours, it was really ridiculous…it was Sodom and Gomorrah."

One of my favorite Chicago Rocked *interviews was with Steve Albini (Performer-Big Black/Rapeman/Shellac; Producer-Nirvana, the Jesus Lizard, etc.). I paid him a visit at the Electrical Audio compound on Belmont, and I thought it went great ... until the end.*

My then-publisher had asked me to get paperwork permission "sign offs" from everyone I spoke to for the book, and I "cold sweat" dreaded asking Albini for his. This was, after all, a guy whose entire career was built on honorable "handshake" agreements.

When I pulled out the one-sheet after the interview, Albini lambasted me for the perceived disrespect and let me find my own way out the door. I wasn't surprised or offended. I did what the publisher asked me to do, and it played out in the exact way I'd expected.

Before things broke bad, Albini shared a lot of articulate, well-studied thoughts on music, the business of music, and the behaviors of bands in the 90s. In this excerpt, he called out the ambitions and motives of the local bands swept up in the major label signing frenzy that hit Chicago in the mid-90s. He had me at "coterie of assholes."

"Every band that operates in that ... sort of mainstream show business idiom eventually develops a coterie of assholes that they have to drag from place to place and pay for at all times. So, while the Smashing Pumpkins were popular and successful, they could afford all of that. Almost all the other bands that tried to behave like that could not afford that, or could only afford it for a very, very short term.

Albini went on to summarize the major label-inspired insanity happening in 1990s Chicago:

"... there's that mode of behavior which had not existed in Chicago up until that point ... and you had a lot of bands operating on that principle. That is, let's get famous first, then worry about being in a band."

Regarding the Pumpkins, in the 90s, they were veritable poster children for the nebulous concept of "Alternative Rock." Their break-up in 2000 gave rise to a Billy Corgan who's been unpredictable, erratic; and at times, just plain bizarro. Consider:

He followed up the Pumpkins with Zwan, a band that didn't survive past the release of their first album.

He released a solo album (The Future Embrace), *but neutered any impact it might have had by taking out a newspaper ad in the* Chicago Tribune *and* Chicago Sun-Times *on the same day, announcing his intention to reunite the Pumpkins.*

He started, and abruptly stopped, a spirituality-based blog.

He released a book of poetry.

He reformed the Pumpkins with Jimmy Chamberlin and two unknowns.

Chamberlin left the band in 2009. I think one or more unknowns were replaced, too, but it doesn't really matter--the Smashing Pumpkins is Corgan's movie; everyone else is just playing a walk-on role.

At press time, the new version of the band is gradually releasing the 44 songs from a new album called Teargarden By Kaleidyscope *for free, online.*

Throughout his career, even at the Pumpkins' upper atmosphere peak, Billy was never one to take criticism lightly.

(September 13, 2010)

Billy Corgan vs. Blogger: A Twitter Opera

Apparently a blogger (newspaper critic?) wrote some negative things about Billy Corgan that warranted a day of

semi-responses via Twitter. I've Googled the bejesus out of
the Pumpkins and Billy today, but for the life of me, I
couldn't pinpoint the offending source.

In any event, what was said struck a major nerve with
the Great Pumpkin. Here are the highlights from Billy's
Twitter:

* Whoever wrote the article here in the local paper about The
Mighty SP is a fucking idiot ... excuse me, I meant to say a
TOTAL FUCKING MORON about 6 hours ago via txt

* I love when some writer tries to put themselves over at my
expense. Really unique concept. I've been here for over 20
years. Your kind=lame about 6 hours ago via txt

* All your silly words can't kill the Love in SP. This band is
going to win and you can't stand it: Mikey, Nicole, Jeff, and
BC are HERE about 6 hours ago via txt

* Actually, to be honest, 3/4 of SP are in Portland. I am in the
woods, in front of a fire cooking up a lovely, earthen brew.
Time is coming.. about 6 hours ago via txt

* Old SP: Dead. Buried. Gone. New SP: Alive. Free.
Dangerous. God: The Best! Absolute. Unconditional.
Radical. about 6 hours ago via txt

* You know those horror movies where there is the *thing* that won't die? That is SP. We a'int (sic) gonna make that mistake again. Hipsters beware! about 3 hours ago via txt

* Hipsters and blog fascists beware because SP exposes that your game isn't real, integral, fair, or even about music. It is about YOU about 3 hours ago via txt

* Show me a band or a music artist with a problem and I will at least bow to them doing *some-thing* in this world, ego or not... about 3 hours ago via txt

* How did the world get so upside down that the people who write about music see themselves as more valuable than the artists themselves? about 3 hours ago via txt

* SP continues to expose the wires to the farce that is the mu-sick biz-ness...thank you to the radio stations that support us as independents about 3 hours ago via txt

* Thank you to the indie retailers who honor the long history of SP and our place in alternative culture. Don't you get it yet? about 3 hours ago via txt

* The Smashing Pumpkins are back. And we a'int going fucking anywhere but UP ha ha fucking hardy har har...what a beautiful day to LOVE+HONOR about 3 hours ago via txt

* Thank you thank you thank you to the Smashing Pumpkins fans who have stuck with us. We appreciate you! Gonna rock you Spokane! about 3 hours ago via txt

* But if you piss on my lawn I'm gonna tell you to get the hell off my lawn.The message hasn't changed since '87. We're in the makeithappenbiz about 1 hour ago via txt

It's like, *news flash*, the circus has elephants+clowns+a guy in a top hat. SP is what it is + it a'int (sic) changing to match your death dream about 1 hour ago via txt

* People change. People move on. People grow up (not me obviously!!). I'm happy. Love Love Love being in this band! I make no apology for us. about 1 hour ago via txt

Billy has a history of letting critics rattle him, dating back to the mid-90s, when then-Sun-Times critic Jim DeRogatis was banned from attending a Pumpkins' Double Door show. DeRogatis' solution was to stand outside the venue on Milwaukee Avenue, and write a review based on what he could hear rattling though the windows and walls. Billy and DeRogatis were like matter and anti-matter; when the two collided, the fabric of the universe threatened to unravel.

Criticism sucks. No one enjoys it, this blogger included. While it's easy to say that an artist shouldn't read his/her own press, that's simply not a realistic practice. Artists want to know whether or not they're striking a chord with the people who are consuming their work. That said, most artists realize that reading reviews and articles come with ego-bruising risk. I don't know what the offending critic wrote, or if the content was needlessly personal, but I'm sure it was ... impolite.

(Easy for me to say), but I think that Corgan should've turned a blind eye to the offending journalist. By devoting his Twitter feed to this blogger/reviewer, Billy has given the critic more attention than he (or she) has likely ever had on the internet (which I'm sort of adding to).

If anyone reading this knows Billy Corgan, please let him know, "Dude, you wrote 'Cherub Rock' and 'I Am One.' ... It's all good ... Let it go ... It just doesn't matter."

RU-USH

CHAPTER FOUR

Let's get this out of the way: I fucking love Rush. My appreciation for the band (Geddy Lee, Alex Lifeson, and Neil Peart) doesn't stop, as it does for many, with the obvious album choices of Moving Pictures *and* Permanent Waves. *My love for the long-running, musically gifted trio spans every one of the band's creative eras.*

*I celebrate and hold in high regard their concept albums (*Hemispheres, 2112*), epic-length songs ("Jacob's Ladder," "Xanadu," "The Fountain of Lamenth"), 80s synth flirtations (c'mon, "Distant Early Warning" rules), and unjustly-ignored material from the 90s and 00s ("Dreamline" and "Far Cry" are two of the best songs they've ever recorded).*

As other Rush fans know, there are times when you have to justify your fandom to non-believers.

(March 8, 2010)

<u>Why Rush?</u>

My pal Jen Jameson got to do a fill-in shift at the Loop (WLUP-FM) today. She made a point of "tweeting" me halfway through her show to tell me that she was playing "The Trees" by Rush. She knows I'm a fan, but probably thinks I'm a dork because of it. It's never been cool to like Rush. Here are three of the commonly-cited reasons why:

"The lead singer sounds like a girl!" Geddy Lee has an unusually high, sometimes screechy, voice, but it's a male voice. It's also a unique voice that seems perfectly suited to conveying the weighty and fantastic lyrics drummer Neal Peart writes.

"Prog rock sucks!" While I'm all for three-minute, three chord catharsis, I also stand behind technically proficient proggers from King Crimson to Dream Theater for intellectual stimulation and novel-length wankery. What's more, side one of *Hemispheres* is good on a level of being life-affirming.

"The lyrics are silly!" They are, when taken out of context. And I hope and pray that the band is someday forgiven for "By-Tor and the Snow Dog." Layered on top of the music,

though, the lyrics are majestic. Socially insightful. Interesting, too.

When Q101 was at its commercial peak in the 90s, I had to deny my Rush urges. Professing a love for Rush back then would've been as jarring to the alt-rock nation as saying "I put the gun in Kurt Cobain's hand."

One year ago this month, it became okay-ish to listen to Rush when the hit film *I Love You, Man* brought Paul Rudd and Jason Segel to the party. Even so, my snarkier, more musically sanctimonious, friends still wouldn't hear any of it. I tried my best to first reel them in with the band's hits, like "Closer to the Heart" and "Tom Sawyer" ("Xanadu" and "Digital Man" are songs that are earned, not given). I pointed out how tight the band is throughout "Spirit of the Radio" ... How "Limelight" may in fact have the greatest guitar riff ever ... How "Subdivisions" speaks to the alienated child in us all. I'm convinced that they wouldn't be swayed because they *chose* not to be swayed.

I'm unapologetically a Rush fan. I've got their library "on shuffle" as I'm writing this. If liking Rush isn't cool, well ... I'm okay with what that makes me.

(December 21, 2006)

<u>Fill 'er Up. With Prog.</u>

I filled my car's gas tank up tonight, cutting off the flow when the total hit $21.12. I figured it'd be easy to remember because A) the number is a palindrome; and B) It's the name of Rush's magnum opus.

That got me thinking about how many other people pull out at the moment of absolute Peartness. Then I started to think that there must be a way for gas stations to sort and rank gas purchases by total spent. I'd imagine that $10 and $20 would be the big winners, with honorable mention given to "$21.12," "$6.66," and "12.34." I then wiped those thoughts from my mind, bought a bag of puffy Cheetos and a Coke Zero, and drove on.

A Rush performance is no typical concert; it's an hours-long commitment, most readily endured by the previously-converted.

I spent most of late Spring, 2010 looking forward to the Chicago stop of Rush's "Time Machine" tour in July. The "Time Machine" tour was special, in that it featured a live performance of the legendary Moving Pictures *album ("Tom Sawyer," "Limelight," "YYZ," "Red Barchetta") on every night on the tour.*

Weather conspired against the band, as driving rain and winds forced a show cancellation minutes after the band was supposed to take the stage. While it sucked to be sent back home only an hour after arriving at the venue, I couldn't argue with the reason why.

Some people were less understanding; one fan decided to sue the band for his inconvenience:

(July 11, 2010)

Rush Show Cancelled Due to Weather: Let's Sue the Fuckers!

Denied. A venue full of Rush fans didn't get the chance perform at the Charter One Pavilion on Wednesday. After two hours of "will they or won't they" speculation during relentless and soul-soaking rain, a Live Nation representative marched out onto the Charter One stage at 8:15 to announce that the show had to be postponed, "for the safety of the audience, and also for the safety of Rush."

Rush fans are nothing, if not civilized. There was great disappointment in the crowd, but the masses marched out of the venue with nary a loud vulgarity or bottle thrown. We were all in sticky plastic ponchos, feet pruned from standing in puddles; we all understood the situation. At least I thought we all did. Based on his (legal) actions, an out-of-town visitor didn't: He decided to file a class action lawsuit against Rush (his favorite band) and Live Nation.

I suspect that I lived through a similar series of circumstances as the litigious fan.

My wife and I got to the Soldier Field parking lot at around 6:30. As we pulled in, the rain was coming down at a steady drizzle. By the time we walked to the lot's walkway exit, the rain was coming down hard ... and sideways.

We decided to wait in the entry way, which was little more than a sweltering concrete bunker, stocked with one sad, overpriced soda machine. About 40 other people were packed in there with us as we all tried to "wait out the rain." At that point, I wasn't convinced that I wanted to stick around. Thoughtful head bobbing in the driving rain for three hours seemed more like a chore than actual fun.

The rain slowed by 7:30. Not stopped, mind you, but slowed enough to be considered "survivable." The showtime was set for 7:30, which I hoped would be a bit delayed because of the weather. We bolted out of the bunker and made our trek from the Soldier Field parking garage to the former Meigs Field.

By the time I got into the Will Call line to pick up my (admittedly kickass) tickets, the rain picked right back up. I was soaked by the time I was handed my envelope.

As we crossed the front gate, we were handed clear plastic ponchos, which we eagerly threw on. Fashion has no place in a rainstorm; even less so at a Rush concert. And while I'm on the subject, there's nothing less appealing than placing warm plastic on one's wet, sweaty body.

I saw (disc jockey) Byrd broadcasting live for the Loop as we walked through the gate, so I stopped to say hello. Byrd's a friendly face, and a fellow Rush fan with whom I've had tons of super-geeky classic rock conversations. He saw the show on Monday, and told me I was "in for a treat."

Once we got to our seats, we looked at the stage to see Rush's equipment covered in plastic sheeting. What's more, there were roadies Shopvac-ing and sweeping water off the stage as best they could. By 7:50, the rain had stopped, and I enthusiastically assumed that my chance to thoughtfully headbob was near. By 8:10, it started to drizzle again. And at 8:15, we got the unfortunate announcement. "Another storm front is set to move in within 30 minutes," the announcer said, offering a reason for the show's postponement. "Save your tickets; they will be honored for the rescheduled date," he added. And with that, we marched back to the Soldier Field lot with the masses, clothes clingy, attitudes dejected.

When I pulled back out of the lot, it started to rain again. It wasn't coming down hard, but it was enough to cause me to have my windshield wipers on for the entire trip home. In the end, Live Nation made a good call in killing the show. Sure, the night cost me some babysitter money. And it's true that I was hell-bent on seeing *Moving Pictures* performed live. But I'll get another chance to see the show; and, in a weird way, the evening was a fun adventure for my wife and me. In short, the night wasn't a total loss.

Back to the guy who initiated legal action, at the core of the lawsuit is the notion of the ticket reading "rain or shine." That's what mine said, too. There's also a mess of super-fine legalese on the backside of the ticket which seems to negate the absolute nature of "rain or shine."

Sometimes, circumstances don't happen in as neat and orderly a way as we'd prefer. This was an extreme circumstance, and an unfortunate one at that. The stage at the Charter One is a far cry (Rush pun intended) from the size of the United Center stage, where the band last played in Chicago. The Charter One stage also has little to no overhead shelter, making outdoor shows in inclement weather a risky proposition.

I certainly understand the frustration of the fans, as I am one of them. I also can appreciate how frustrating it must've been for an out-of-town visitor. This isn't cataclysmic stuff, though. In non-legal terms, shit happens. As it did on Wednesday.

Chicago Breaking News quoted the lawsuit as saying, "The White Sox completed a game in the weather in Chicago on the evening of July 7, 2010," as if the Sox/Angels game and Rush concert are analogous. Consider:

The guys in Rush wear wireless electronic equipment.

The Charter One stage was covered in water.

For the better part of the night, the rain came in sideways.

It was great that the Sox were able to play (#1 team in the AL Central right now, thankyouverymuch), but there's no reasonable way to make an "apples to apples" comparison between a ball game and an outdoor rock show.

The ham-fisted approach for restitution makes me wonder what other options the plaintiff tried before filing a class action lawsuit against his favorite band. Did he contact LiveNation, local or national? Did he contact the Better Business Bureau? Rush management? Did he realize, as a Rush fan, that the band takes its fans seriously, and deeply regrets situations like this?

Finally, if I were visiting Chicago with a bunch of buddies for the night/week/whatever, I'm confident that I could find plenty to do in town to make it so that my airfare and trip to the Windy City weren't completely wasted.

And if I couldn't? Well, then, I'd just sue anyone who disrupted the way the world rotates in its axis around good old, self-important me.

This lawsuit just plain offends me.

A rescheduled show happened just a few weeks later at the same venue.

(October, 29, 2009/Twitter)

<u>Lost in Ontario</u>

Somehow got lost inside Toronto's airport campus. YYZ is no longer my favorite Rush instrumental.

The Time Machine Tour kept going into 2011, and found its way back to Chicago on 4/12/11, when the band headlined the massive United Center.

The show was a song-for-song duplicate of what I'd seen eight months before. What was different when I went to the show this time is that I had "meet and greet" passes to meet the band before the show.

This is the sort of opportunity that longtime fans would make incredible sacrifices for. Once I confirmed that I had the access, I could barely contain my excitement.

Unfortunately, my time with Rush was more disappointing than if I'd never even had the opportunity in the first place.

(April 15, 2011)

<u>My Three Seconds With Rush</u>

I had a "once in a lifetime" moment this week: I met Rush. I met them during a backstage "meet and greet" about an hour before the start of their show at the United Center.

Meet and greets are (usually) small, organized gatherings where fans (almost always contest winners and people who "know somebody") meet famous people. As a rule, they're awkward, rushed affairs which allow fans to have a few minutes of interaction with their heroes and then get one or two treasured items signed.

These events aren't like meeting the band at a corner bar--meet and greet environments are controlled, usually shoehorned into a vacant dressing room. Security, record, and management personnel are always on hand to keep things moving along, and to keep the fans from being creepy. It's like going on a blind date where the girl's parents are sitting at the next table over as you eat dinner.

I've been fortunate enough to have attended a few meet and greets in my career, though Rush was the first one I'd been to in over six years. The best meet and greets are those where the band tries to engage with its fans and is humble enough to accept the effusive praise they receive. The members of Metallica, for instance, go out of their way to make every visitor feel special, even the more casual fans in the room.

Based on Rush's "everyman," wholesome persona, I expected a friendly, congenial, environment. And without a doubt, I came ready to meet my favorite band: I brought a digital camera and a vinyl copy of *2112* to have the band sign in silver ink.

When I arrived at the venue, I was issued a document with the following information:

Now that you have picked up your tickets and/or passes, please proceed to **CONCOURSE AREA ACROSS FROM SECTION 119-120 ENTRANCE, UNDER THE HINCKLEY SPRINGS WATER SIGN, WHERE YOU WILL BE MET BY SECURITY. BE THERE NO LATER THAN 6:30.** We are on a very tight schedule, and unfortunately cannot accommodate latecomers.

Tonight we will be taking pictures of you with the band. If you have brought your own camera, please put it away, as you will not need it, nor will we allow you to use it.

Unfortunately, we will not have time for autographs tonight, so if you have anything to be autographed, please leave it in the car, or keep it put away.

You will be coming in and getting an photograph with the guys, and then you will be directed back out. Your photograph will be very high quality, and within 24 hours you can go to www.rush.com/picturetime to retrieve your pictures.

To the contest winners-Congratulations!
To the fans-Thank you for being there all these years!

The information on the sheet is the same for every market, save the exception of the specific night's precise location and time, which were written in bold.

After reading the instructions, it was clear that my short-term goal of owning a matted and framed autographed Rush album would never be realized.

While I'm on the topic: 2112 is a legendary album--in general, as well as in the Rush discography. It's not solely because of the music, either: the cover artwork is iconic. The "star" image and "2112" logo have an indelible place in rock history.

As indelible as the front cover is, the back cover photo is 1970s awfulness. Since childhood, I've had to forgive the band for their kimonos and Alex Lifeson's split camel toe. Related: ouch.

Back to the meet and greet: as we waited backstage to meet the band, a representative for Rush addressed the room and reinforced the details spelled out on the instruction sheet. As he explained, violating any of the rules would result in things getting real ugly, real fast. "Geddy (Lee) and Alex (Lifeson) will come in and stand in front of a backdrop," he said. "At that point, we'll invite you and the group you came with to take a picture with the guys. Once your picture's taken, you'll need to leave the room."

Rush has a photographer who shoots the meet and greets and later posts the images online. There's your keepsake souvenir, boys and girls--go to Rush.com tomorrow to hunt for yours.

When my friend and I were summoned, we shook hands with Alex and Geddy. I said "nice to meet you" to them both, and then my friend and I moved into place for our photo opportunity. In an instant, the picture was taken and we were shown the door.

I want to be emphatically clear about this next point: I was truly fortunate to have had the meet and greet opportunity in the first place, and to have exchanged handshakes with the band. As much as I try to remind myself of that, though, I can't help but feel hollow about the experience. Alex and Geddy didn't say a single word back to me.

This begs the question: why does Rush even agree to meet and greets at all? It can't be fun for them: they get whisked into a room where they stand like mannequins in front of a gathering of strangers who they never once talk to. Then they force smiles for a series of identical wham-bam photos. Once the photo ops are over, they get escorted back to the security and anonymity of their dressing room. Not once does the band get to share in the joy or exuberance the fans are feeling. If I were in a band, meet and greets like that would leave me totally jaded (or would at least encourage me to write a song like "Limelight").

I have no heart to lie.
I can't pretend a stranger
Is a long-awaited friend.

"HATE" IS AN UGLY WORD. AND YET ...

CHAPTER FIVE

Everyone has a band that rubs him the wrong way. For me, that band is Red Hot Chili Peppers. They are the Luthor to my Superman, the Sinestro to my Green Lantern, and the Attuma to my Prince Namor, the Sub-Mariner.

(March 6, 2008)

<u>The Worst Band Ever</u>

I've listened to a lot of music in my lifetime. For every transcendent, life-affirming artist I've heard, I've heard thousands of truly awful, shouldn't-be-allowed-to-buy-an-instrument bands. The awfulness of many of the wretched masses isn't even subject to question or cross-examination. Nickelback? That's a given. Doobie Brothers? Try and come up with an argument for them. I promise you won't win: "Jesus is Just Alright" ... "What a Fool Believes" ... "Old Black Water" ... The only positive thing I can say about the Doobie Brothers is, "well, at least they're not Bob Seger."

Trying to defend my opinions becomes more problematic when an artist is well-loved or well-received by critics. Take, for example, the Beastie Boys. They were a hugely successful act for 20 years. Critics still use the word "seminal" to describe 1989's *Paul's Boutique*. And yet, I can't listen to them for more than a song without feeling as though I've been had. They're a scam ... there's nothing there ... as empty a listening experience as I can imagine (though I do like the first five seconds of "Sabotage").

Then there's Radiohead. Back when *O.K. Computer* came out, I boldly said on the air that the people who were calling it a "masterpiece" probably wouldn't be listening to it five, let alone ten, years later. Apparently I was wrong on that one. I took a lot of crap for it, too. People still love the band, even though their albums have long since hit the point of diminishing returns (*Hail to the Thief*, anyone?). I've tried to listen on multiple occasions, and my conclusion remains: *O.K. Computer* is a torturous album to listen to.

What makes a horrible band horrible? If you're Nickelback, being horrible is what you are; you don't aspire to be anything more. A KIA will always be a KIA. It never pretends to offer the same luxuries as a Mercedes.

It's the truly terrible bands that have fooled the public into believing that they're anything but bad that I hold in greater contempt. For years, I believed that Sonic Youth was a great band. I was told they were. My friends said so. Fanzines said so. *Rolling Stone* and *Spin* said so. What did it matter if *Daydream Nation* was ungraspable noise? I told myself that I obviously didn't get it; the level Sonic Youth played at was beyond my understanding. Several years and a few emotional growth spurts later, I realize there was nothing to get. Sonic Youth has one of the greatest self-indulgent-noisemaking-to-critical-accolade ratios in the history of rock.

As I started to think more about this topic, I concluded that I needed a mathematical way to determine the worst band ever. Here's the formula I applied to over 50 artists I think are terrible (but the world doesn't), including Linkin Park, the Offspring, Hole, Steely Dan, My Chemical Romance, Incubus, the Eagles, Duran Duran, Phish, Poison, Weezer, and ZZ Top. I ranked them all as equal, assigning them all a round number of 10. I then added the total from this formula to each one to account for some of the mitigating factors I addressed above:

(total years of releasing albums) + (total number of average-to-above-average albums) / (total number of albums) + (total

number of top fifty singles on either the mainstream chart or
a relevant genre chart)

Divided by:

(popularity index--determined by five factors including
ticket sales, historical radio airplay, total mainstream
magazine covers, MTV airplay, and "cultural vibe") + (total
of 4 + 5 star reviews in three major music magazines, ten
major alternative press titles, and five major market
newspapers)

=Total

_____

I spent the first two weeks of March crunching the
numbers, and was surprised by the outcome.

The worst band ever? The Red Hot Chili Peppers.

When you think about it, it just makes sense. There's
nothing about them that's not cringeworthy. Their 80s
material is tossed-off frat boy funk. Their 90s material is
hilariously sincere. Their 00's albums are just cash-in repeats
of what they did successfully in the 90s (specifically *Blood
Sugar Sex Magik* and *Californication*).

Can the result be argued? I don't think so. This is math
and science at work. Can you build a right triangle and
violate the Pythagorean Theorem? Can electrostatic force be
explained without using Coulomb's Law?

Ah, Red Hot Chili Peppers. You've given us so much ...
"Party on Your Pussy" (1987) ... five different versions of
"Under the Bridge" ("By the Way," "Scar Tissue," "Otherside,"

"Snow," "My Friends") ... the eight minute-plus "Sir Psycho Sexy" (1991) ... you've earned it. You really do suck.

Update, 5/7/11. Though the Red Hot Chili Peppers continue to suck serious donkey dick, I spent much of my day giving serious consideration to Primus being the worst band ever.

(October 1, 2004)

The Case Against Scott Stapp

I never liked (Creed frontman) Scott Stapp. He always came across as an unlikable, humorless, self-righteous poseur, both on and off stage. With leather pants and nary a smile on his face, he'd strike messianic poses in concert that just screamed out for a beer bottle to make contact with his skull. Creed was not a *fun* band to see live. Granted, the intellectual music fan in me said that the band was comprised of tight, talented players, but I never could get past Stapp.

It was the same thing with Limp Bizkit. I knew Borland was a talented guy; but Durst? Forget about it.

Hole? Same thing.

Frontpeople can absolutely kill a band for me. Fast forward to 2004. Stapp's gone on his biblical vision quest, and Alter Bridge (Creed – Stapp + Myles Kennedy) is rocketing towards a legit career. In their first-ever Chicago show at HOB last night, singer Myles Kennedy felt so much more *real* than Stapp ever did. He was humble, genuine, and soulful, with a vocal range that Stapp can only pray to hit. And, yes, these guys can play.

Last night, the band was professional without the polish that shines up much of the debut CD. The show felt raw, even unpredictable at moments (as when they brought a fan on stage to sing "happy birthday" to her).

Stappless Creed? Works for me. I've embraced it with … sorry …arms wide open.

(June 15, 2004)

<u>I Hate Hippies</u>

Two fans died at the Bonnaroo music festival over the weekend. Investigator Dale Brissey commented, "The high humidity, high heat, alcohol and drugs-it's not a good combination."

I heard the news of the two deaths just half a day after I talked with a good friend of mine about Bonnaroo. He was covering the event for another media company, and was there for the duration. He told me that, in all his concert-going life, he'd never seen as much drug use as was at that event. By his estimation, everyone in the area, including people working the event, were either smoking pot or using hallucinogenics at some point or another over the weekend. I suppose that's to be expected when you're staring at a lineup that includes acts like Trey Anastasio, the Dead, and Government Mule. Jam bands in the great outdoors tend to drive the Abercrombie kids to all sorts of Woodstock-era indulgences.

Forget the potential physical harm for a moment. Forget the illegality, too. Let's just focus on how stupid these people look at these shows. I've seen the Dead (with Jerry), and I've seen plenty other jam bands, too, from String Cheese Incident through O.A.R. I've seen the stretched-out pupils of neo-hippies wacked out from psilocybin-drenched mushrooms. I've seen the same crowd so dramatically cloud their brains with THC, they can barely remember their names, let alone their home addresses. Add a jam band to that cocktail, and you have a host of embarrassing dancing and pseudo, high-minded love for one's fellow man.

As my friend recounted some of his stories--from the cartoon-themed fiefdoms, through the hackeysack-kicking masses--the only feeling I could muster was, "glad I wasn't there." A bunch of suburban kids migrating to Tennessee to drop acid and listen to bongo solos is a scene straight out of Dante's Inferno.

(January 12, 2005)

So Much for the Debt-I-Owe

Art Alexakis of Everclear reportedly filed for Chapter 11 protection last week, having amassed more debt than he can possibly pay. A very petty part of me, a part I'm not proud of, is happy about this.

Let me backtrack. I've been remarkably fortunate in my ten+ years in Chicago radio to have met and interviewed hundreds of musicians. Of all those I've met and/or interviewed, I can count on one hand those who were absolute douchebags. Art Alexakis tops the list.

I had the chance to interview him four times, all during the *Sparkle and Fade* and *So Much For The Afterglow* eras. He was rude, condescending, adversarial, and belligerent every single time. He treated interviews like combat, even in my early days of interviewing when I was more interested in ass-kissing than doing interviews of substance.

He was a bitter, mean, petty, small, and unhappy man every time we shared the same space. It was as if he went out of his way to make me miserable. In contrast, Craig and Greg from Everclear were always a pleasure to deal with.

As I've mentioned time again, you can personally hate an artist (Courtney Love, I'm looking at you), but still like their music. To that end, I still enjoy the following Everclear songs:

> "Nervous and Weird"
> "Summerland"
> "Heroin Girl"

"Fire Maple Song"
"So Much For The Afterglow"
"Heartspark Dollarsign"

It's important to point out that I interviewed Art twice since I originally wrote that in 2005. On both occasions, he was the exact opposite of the belligerent ghoul I first portrayed him to be.

In fact, the interview I did with him on Q101 in June, 2006 stands as one of my favorites.

(February 17, 2011/Twitter)

No, No, No

"Bang" by Yeah Yeah Yeahs just appeared on my iPod. This very well may be the worst song ever made.

*

(February 18, 2011/Twitter)

Radiohead releases new album

Life's much easier when you don't have to pretend to like Radiohead. Join me on the dark side of popular opinion, won't you?

Aging into my (gasp) fourth decade has allowed me to look back on songs and albums I had once reviled with a new sense of open-mindedness.

(April 2, 2009)

Genesis *Calling All Stations*

The Genesis album *Calling All Stations* has been shunned for over a decade now, mostly for committing the alleged sin of not having Phil Collins on it.

Phil Collins made a very clear (and financially incontestable) decision early in the early '80s that he was going to be a full-on pop songwriter and singer. That fact was hammered home by the sounds heard on his second and third solo albums, *Hello, I Must Be Going* and *No Jacket Required*. Naturally, it was only a matter of time before that overt pop sensibility bled over to the band that made Collins a star.

Genesis was certainly no stranger to pop success. "Turn it On Again" and "Misunderstanding" continue to stand out as gems from the Collins days, and are as good as any of the more complex and confounding of the band's works. The difference was that, before *Invisible Touch* (1986), the pop songs always seemed balanced out by the more "Genesissier" songs. For every "Misunderstanding," there was a "Behind the Lines;" for every "No Reply at All," a "Me and Sarah Jane." However, once "In Too Deep," "Throwing It All Away," and "Invisible Touch" made it into the Genesis song library, the transformation of Genesis into unapologetic pop superstars was complete.

Following *Invisible Touch* was 1991's *We Can't Dance*, an album that felt overly sweet and inauthentic. In a word, saccharin. We can all thank Nirvana for providing us with a mighty distraction that particular year.

Six years later, and one year after Collins left the band for good (at least until the inevitable reunion in the late '00s), Genesis returned with an all-new album (*Calling All Stations*) and an all-new ... and mostly unknown ... singer named Ray Wilson.

The album stiffed harder than critics had anticipated. The U.K. was more forgiving, but only because they tend to be a more polite people.

On its own, and separated from the expectations and weight of the Genesis brand, *Calling All Stations* plays like a lighter version of the late '80s, post-Roger Waters, David Gilmour-led, Pink Floyd. Or at least a ballsier Mike and the Mechanics.

There are a handful of songs worth listening to. "Congo" is pretty great, as is the title track. I can sit through all of the near-eight minutes of "The Dividing Line" without clicking my iPod forward. In fact, if not for some scorn-worthy ballads ("Not About Us" being the most egregious), *Calling All Stations* might have had a shot. If not a shot at success, at least a shot at some Genesis cred.

(April 13, 2009)

Billy Joel "Sometimes a Fantasy"

Sing us a song, you're Billy Joel.

There's nothing all that "cool" about the man who gave the world "Just the Way You Are" and "Uptown Girl," except perhaps "Sometimes a Fantasy," from his ginormously successful *Glass Houses* LP.

This track has everything I could ever ask for in a song: Billy Joel channeling Elvis, phone sex frustration, and the most infectiously passive sing-a-long chorus ever (whoa-oh-whoa-oh).

And are those rototoms heard at the 3:17 mark? That clinches it.

(April 19, 2009)

"Science Fiction/Double Feature"

I never "got" "Rocky Horror," though I suppose I put in the effort. Growing up in the north 'burbs, my high school friends and I made frequent weekend trips to the Randhurst Theater for the midnight show. They were trips that were taken more out of the need to find a place to be drunk and obnoxious after 12 a.m., and less of the need to "Time Warp" again. Worse, the experience was usually littered with scads of local acting failures who used the midnight cult cinema experience as a way to vindicate themselves for a lifetime of roles along the lines of "Tree #2."

I have two lasting memories of the movie: First, Susan Sarandon looked fabulous when she was younger. Second, the film's opening song raised the bar far too high for everything else that unspooled over the following 100 minutes. Sung by "Rocky" creator Richard O'Brien, "Science Fiction/Double Feature" is a moody trip through the glory days of B-movies, name-checking the key players of the era, from Fay Wray (*King Kong*) to Michael Rennie (*The Day the Earth Stood Still*. The original). The arrangement is stripped down and haunted, its lyrics reading like the "We Didn't Start the Fire" of '50s horror and sci-fi.

Sliced off of the celluloid cheese it's forever linked with, "Science Fiction/Double Feature" can be heard as an acoustic goth love song to a simpler time when the A-bomb loomed on the horizon and a movie theater could provide ridiculous and fantastic diversion. More simply put, it's worth reevaluating. If you're looking for it *on The Rocky Horror Picture Show* soundtrack, it's just a jump to the left of that other song.

SICK, SAD, MAN:
MICHAEL JACKSON

CHAPTER SIX

When Michael Jackson died on June 25, 2009, I was floored by the revisionist history that was being discussed on television, radio, and web, as well as what was being discussed socially among my friends. Jackson was damaged goods, and almost certainly a pedophile (though never formally convicted). If we, as a society, can't suffer through a Gary Glitter song because of his atrocities, the post-mortem deification of Jackson makes no sense at all.

Leading up to his death, Jackson's life in the early 00s was a traveling circus, and almost always newsworthy for the wrong reasons.

(Wednesday, July 21, 2004)

Mike's Expecting Four

Michael Jackson's back in the news, with *Us Weekly* claiming that he's expecting quadruplets from a surrogate mother in Miami. This is yet another reminder that Michael needs to go away, far away. Not to an unsupervised place, either. Mike, we as a society are done with you. Hope you enjoy your stay in the "sodomy wing" of the state lockup. Thanks for "Billie Jean," but we're moving on now, you sick, sad, messed up freak.

(Friday, February 4, 2005)

Slaying the King of Pop

I was thinking about the Michael Jackson case today. I realize he won't be eligible for the death penalty, but if he were, would executing him be considered regicide? He is the king of pop, after all.

Michael Jackson was arrested on molestation, conspiracy, and alcohol charges in 2003. When he failed to show up to court in March, 2005, a bench warrant was issued for his arrest.

(March 10, 2005 11:28am)

Bench Warrant: Beat it

I'm in the studio, watching CNN as the clock ticks down for Michael Jackson to beat his bench warrant. This is better than "24!" Depending on the outcome, it might even be better viewing than the O.J. chase.

(March 10, 2005 11:42am)

Bench Warrant: Dangerous

Deadline has passed. Jackson was just walked into the courtroom. Fans outside the courthouse chanted encouragement as he walked past. Who are these ghouls offering encouragement to the dethroned king of pop? It's unthinkable to me. I've gotta think even the most ardent Jackson supporters might want to hedge their bets, and wait to see if he becomes a convicted child molester before voicing their support.

When Jackson beat the rap in 2005, he managed to avoid 20 years in prison.

As it turned out, some people had in fact hedged their bets before allowing themselves to "like" Mike again.

(June 22, 2005)

It's safe to buy Michael Jackson CDs again

It's so...creepy...that after a long absence, Michael Jackson's *Number Ones* CD reappeared on the Top 200 albums this week. It's as though people were waiting to buy it until they found out whether he was going to be a convicted child molester or not.

After his court victory, Michael spent the ensuing years slipping into prescribed comas, mostly falling off my radar. And then…

(June 25, 2009)

<u>The King is Dead</u>

The internet practically collapsed into itself, dwarf star-like, upon hearing the TMZ-leaked news of Michael Jackson's death. Suddenly, all work in my office stopped, the staff responding like the war room at CNN after a terrorist attack on domestic soil.

To be fair, I joined right in.

The thing about Facebook, you learn pretty quick who your funny friends are. Some of the comments I read after the first cardiac arrest report, and then immediately after the death announcement, were ultra-serious ("thanks for inspiring me in my youth," "what a talent ..."). The ones that I enjoyed most were those that were honest, unfiltered, and absolutely of the moment. Within 15 minutes of the TMZ story breaking, my Facebook home page displayed the following:

"…thinks little boys across the world are cheering like the Ewoks after the Emperor died."

"Holy Shit Ed McMahon Died!?! WTF"

"michael jackson died, maybe, twitter explodes"

"I know Farrah has died and Michael Jackson had a heart attack, but way to run it out Konerko"

The last one was from Steve Dahl, who I'm fake friends with on Facebook (as opposed to the people I actually do know on Facebook but have zero real-life correspondence with). Thinking about Dahl made me think about radio. Thinking about radio got me fired up to get in the car after work and hear the on-air chatter about Jacko.

I got in my car at around 5:50 and turned on the radio. The result? I must've just missed hearing about it on WBBM-AM. I tuned in before and during their national news at the top of the hour and heard everything but the Jackson story. Jack-FM? They would need an actual air personality first. XRT? I've got to assume they at least mentioned it, but I got stuck in one of their endless stopsets. I was, however, excited to learn that Buddy Guy, Guster, and Booker T. are doing their July 4th show. Cool bill. The Drive was elbow-deep in music, and once they go in that direction they don't come back up for a while. Same situation with the Loop at that moment. Then I bounced over to Q101. Sure enough, the first thing I heard was the Manno Brothers talking about it, and then playing "Thriller" out of the conversation. I would have expected to hear "Smooth Criminal" by Alien Ant Farm on Q101 ... not the Full Jacko.

Credit to the station—this is what I understand good radio to be. "Pattern break" moments are resonant and meaningful to the audience, and are almost totally absent from the air these days. Off-topic discussions or disruptions that take a listener out of his comfort zone help bond the listener to the personality, and keep the station sounding fresh and vital. I hate "Thriller." I've hated it for close to thirty years. But I'll remember that Q101 played it tonight. Topical and refreshing. Well done.

VALHALLA: ROCK DEATHS

CHAPTER SEVEN

Speaking of music deaths, here's a smattering of things I said when other musicians passed:

(December 12, 2007)

Ike Turner

Ike Turner was an ex-con. A drug abuser. A well-storied (in film, no less) spouse abuser (though he's always denied it). Ike Turner checked out today at the age of 76.

I'm grateful for "Rocket 88"and all, but Ike was always a scumbag; the kind of performer who reinforces my belief that you can appreciate an artist's art, but shouldn't automatically appreciate that artist.

As it is in "real life," the world of entertainment is littered with self-important dicks, bozos, and people who should never be thought of as role models. I love David Bowie's *Station to Station* album, but when I heard an interview with him saying that he doesn't even remember recording it because he was so messed up on cocaine, my opinion of him dropped dramatically (later Bowie releases like *Never Let Me Down* and the two Tin Machine albums only made things worse).

Kurt Cobain was an extraordinarily gifted songwriter. He also did heroin and killed himself, knowingly leaving a child and shrew behind. Again–great art, not so much as a role model.

Motley Crue? Not even great art (though I'll cop to loving that riff from "Too Fast For Love" and most of the *Dr. Feelgood* album). While their autobiographical *The Dirt* reads like overblown parody, the stories are real, and those stories were told by arrogant, snotty, and aimless jerkoffs who should praise their personal gods daily for the fact that they're still alive.

Ike Turner's "Rocket 88" was etched into rock and roll's Rosetta Stone. His duets with Tina still manage to give me chills. But I still urge caution before we as a society canonize the man, now that he's passed.

One of the more fun aspects of working in radio programming is booking talent for station events and concerts. When I was Music Director at "The Zone," I was ecstatic to have helped book a morning show broadcast that featured Anthrax, Saliva, Kenny Wayne Shepherd, and Damage Plan.

What made Damage Plan an exciting addition was the fact that it was a brand new band for ex-Pantera siblings and for-real metal heroes Vinnie Paul and Dimebag Darrell.

Two nights before the event, the Zone's night host, Matt Wright, called to let me know that Dimebag Darrell had been murdered. He was gunned down on stage, only seconds after Damage Plan had started their show in Columbus, Ohio.

(Thursday, December 9, 2004)

<u>Dimebag Darrell</u>

I was almost asleep last night when the phone rang around 11. No one ever calls me that late, so I naturally assumed it was bad news. And it was.

The Dimebag Darrell murder last night was shocking, unprecedented (as far as I know) in the history of rock. It's impossible to imagine being in the crowd, witnessing homicides live on stage.

How deranged was the guy whose voices drove him to that horrible act? How damaged must a human being's psyche be to even consider such a thing?

I've heard lots of people talk about this being "horrible loss for the metal community," but honestly, the impact of Dime's killing is bigger than that.

The murder is a horrible loss for music, the rock community, and the sense of safety we all instinctively feel when we come together as fans at a show.

What an absolute tragedy.

(January 3, 2011)

Gerry Rafferty

Sad news: Gerry Rafferty, the Scotsman who sang "Stuck in the Middle With You" (Stealers Wheel) and created one of my favorite hits of the 70s ("Baker Street") died at the age of 63 today.

Listening to "Baker Street" and "Right Down the Line" throws me back in time, straight into the back seat of my parent's car, listening to those songs on WLS in the mid-70s. Sad trombone? Not today. Sad sax.

One of the more chilling music deaths of the still-new 21st century was the triple homicide of three Chicago-based musicians on July 14, 2005.

Doug Meis (Exo, The Dials), John Glick (The Returnables), and Michael Dahlquist (Silkworm) were sitting at a traffic light in the middle of the day when a suicidal woman intentionally rammed their car at high speed, killing all three musicians. In a cruel twist, their killer survived.

She was paroled in 2008.

(Thursday August 4, 2005)

Chicago musicians Doug Meis, John Glick, and Michael Dahlquist

This past weekend, I drove by the site in Skokie where three local musicians (Doug Meis, John Glick, and Michael Dahlquist) were murdered a few weeks back.

To recap: a woman bent on killing herself turned her car into a high-speed weapon and aimed it at another car to get the job done. She alone survived the brutal impact.

Some flowers and a small poster board tribute remain where the incident happened on the corner of Niles Center Road and Dempster. The whole thing chilled me to the bone when I first heard about it, and I've had a hard time properly expressing the gravity of the loss on my "Local Zone" show (WZZN). The murder was so sad, so tragic, so stupid, and so completely inhuman, it's impossible to come up with the right thing to say on the radio.

It was a strange, hard-to-define, sense of "local music connectedness" that led me north to the murder site on Sunday. And, looking back, I don't know what I was planning to do once I got there. But I went. Sitting at the red light, I felt sick to my stomach as I imagined how the nightmare played out.

As for the murderer, there's no punishment severe enough for having selfishly inflicted this kind of unnecessary loss.

Quick hits from my blog and Twitter after learning the news of other music-related deaths:

(May 21, 2010/Twitter)

Headed downtown, listening to the Holy Diver album (Dio). R.I.P., you Satanic, big-voiced, little man.

*

(December 25, 2006)

James Brown dead: I feel neutral.

*

(June 10, 2004)

Ray Charles is dead. What I'd Say about that would hardly be adequate to properly address the man's legacy.

COVER SONGS

CHAPTER EIGHT

I'm a sucker for cover songs. To keep my enjoyment of covers going, I decided to lay down some cover rules in '04:

(Thursday, November 11, 2004)

<u>JAMES VANOSDOL'S COVER SONG GROUND RULES</u>

I went to Joe's last night to see Magna-Fi.

Just a thought-one cover in a set for a nationally touring act is okay. Two is dangerous. Three is, well, far too many. The band pounded out the holy trinity of old rock last night-"Highway to Hell," "Crazy Train," and "Hot For Teacher."

After that, I felt it was important to lay down cover song ground rules for this and future generations of musicians:

1. Only one cover per set, played as an encore. Unless ...

1a. The cover is largely unknown or obscure. An obscure song can go anywhere in the set. No one will know the difference.

2. If the cover is well-known, as in the case of "Crazy Train," the band either has to ...

2a. Completely reinvent the song, make it their own. Or ...

2b. Deliver it in a boozed up, raunchy, sort of way to make it seem like a crazy, drunken whim.

3. Certain songs are sacrosanct and should never be covered, even in an effort to be ironic-"Stairway to Heaven," "Smells Like Teen Spirit," etc.

4. None of these rules apply if you're a band that exists in the megastar stratosphere. Dylan, Metallica, U2, Springsteen, et al, can and will do whatever they want.

Powerglove is one of the most ridiculous bands I've ever seen play live; they're a metal band that plays nothing but covers of videogame and cartoon theme songs. *I had no idea what they were all about before they took the stage at Metro in Chicago, though I figured it out pretty fast. Here's the stream of tweets from my first Powerglove experience:*

(March 15, 2010)

* Powerglove on stage: "We're going to take you to the land of Wolverine ... this ... is ...' X-Men.'" Best and worst opening band ever.

* Oh, I get it ... they do videogame and cartoon themes. Groan.

*... and that's why they're dressed like Bowzer. Tetris theme: check. Mortal Kombat: check.

* I will continue to hate on Powerglove until they play Dig Dug or Burger Time.

* If I were Hammerfall, I'd never let a videogame/cartoon cover band open for me. People wonder why the public doesn't take metal seriously ...

* Powerglove makes *This is Spinal Tap* look like *Precious*.

* They ended the show by saying "game over" and covering the Power Rangers theme. I hate myself so much right now.

Exclusively created for this book, here's my list of 30 can't-miss, indispensable, cover songs:

1. "Tainted Love" (Gloria Jones/Soft Cell)
2. "Ring of Fire" (Johnny Cash/Social Distortion)
3. "Hazy Shade of Winter" (Simon & Garfunkel/The Bangles)
4. "I Fought the Law" (The Crickets/The Clash)
5. "Take Me to the River" (Al Green/Talking Heads)
6. "Jump" (Van Halen/Aztec Camera)
7. "Stagger Lee" (Mississippi John Hurt/Nick Cave and the Bad Seeds)
8. "John the Revelator" (trad./Depeche Mode)
9. "I Want Candy" (The Strangeloves/Bow Wow Wow)
10. "Got the Time" (Joe Jackson/Anthrax)
11. "Don't Leave Me This Way" (Harold Melvin & the Blue Notes/Communards)
12. "Superman" (The Clique/R.E.M.)
13. "Love Her Madly" (The Doors/Wailing Souls)
14. "Do Ya Think I'm Sexy?" (Rod Stewart/Revolting Cocks)
15. "Sweet Child O' Mine" (Guns N' Roses/Aluminum Group)
16. "Money" (Barrett Strong/The Flying Lizards)
17. "Wonderwall" (Oasis/The Mike Flowers Pops)
18. "Mad World" (Tears for Fears/Gary Jules)
19. "Black Steel" (Public Enemy/Tricky)
20. "Memories Can't Wait" (Talking Heads/Living Colour)

21. "All Along the Watchtower (Bob Dylan/Jimi Hendrix Experience)

22. "Hurdy Gurdy Man" (Donovan/Butthole Surfers)

23. "Custard Pie" (Led Zeppelin/Helmet with David Yow)

24. "Ever Fallen In Love" (Buzzcocks/The Noisettes)

25. "Common People" (Pulp/William Shatner)

26. "Mysterious Ways" (U2/KMFDM)

27. "Sweet Jane" (Velvet Underground/Cowboy Junkies)

28. "(I'm Not Your) Stepping Stone" (The Monkees/Sex Pistols)

29. "Pictures of Matchstick Men" (Status Quo/Camper Van Beethoven)

30. "Temptation" (Heaven 17/Cradle of Filth)

WORDPLAY

CHAPTER NINE

Wordplay and puns have a habit of consuming my creative energies for days on end, much to my wife's disapproval. Here's one such example:

(February 26, 2010)

<u>Bands as Food</u>

About a week ago, I noticed a tweet from my pal, Felix. He'd transformed band names into "food band" names. Since then, I've been firing off my own names on Twitter as they've popped in my head. I've decided to collect them here for clarity's sake:

Against Miso

Alice Grouper

Allison Soyet

Allspice Girls

Anthrax of Lamb

Baking Benjamin

Bananowar

Beef BourguignYanni

Beignet Lee

Berry Lee Lewis

Big Head Todd and the Flan-sters

Bill Buffet-ley and the Comets

Bjork Chops

Blue Cheer-ios

Blue Octoburger

Bruce Springrollsteen

Buffalo Wing Springfield

CaraMel Torme

Carly Pie-mon

Celene Dijon

Chauhaus

Chili Nelson

Chop Suey Lewis and the News

Dinos'more Jr.

Donut Hole Surfers

Dr. Dragel

Eatwood Mac / Fleetwood Snack / Fleetwood Big Mac

Electric Light Porkestra

Elvis Cos-Jello

Elvis Parsley

Four Tapas

Frank Zapple

Golden Graham Earring

Green Daysin Bran

Hot Hot Meat

Husker Stew (Stewsker Du?)

Judas Feast

Kenny Wayne Shepherd's Pie

Low-Cal H

My Morning Snacket

Naked Filetgun

Nat King Cole Slaw

Nick Cave and the Sunflower Seeds

Peter, Bjorn, and Hoppin' John

PBJ Harvey

Queso Fun-Dido

Ravio-Lee Scratch Perry

Red Jumpsuit Apple-Ratus

Salmon and Dave

Sigur Gyros

Slim Jimbaland

Soup Dogg

Stabbing Chicken Breastward

Sunny Day Meal Estate

Ted Nougat

Three Days Grapes

TL-Seafood

Toastla

Tofu Fighters

Tragically Chip

Urge Popoverkill

Veal Young

Velveeta Underground

Yolk Explosion

*In 2011, I found myself looking back on the fun I had as a
dumb junior high kid, going downtown with friends to see live
wrestling cards. I hadn't given wrestling much thought over the
past 20+ years, but once I opened the floodgates, it got ugly.*

(February 18, 2011)

Pro Wrestling and Rock and Roll

I haven't watched professional wrestling since 1985. I
was a high school sophomore at that point, and my social
life was screaming for me to grow out of it and move
forward.

Up until then, I had been a hardcore fan. My friends and
I made frequent trips to the UIC Pavilion to see monthly
AWA cards featuring superstars like The Fabulous
Freebirds, the Road Warriors, George "The Animal" Steele,
Baron von Raschke, and Jesse "The Body" Ventura. We made
posters, we bought the programs, and we loved every
minute.

I was pretty aware of the fact that everything I saw was
pure theater, but that didn't bug me. It was like watching
comic book heroes and villains come to life, only bloodier.

Once I made up my mind to leave wrestling behind, no
distraction could take me off point. I had no interest, for
instance, in the initial round of Wrestlemanias. Not even
Hulk Hogan vs. King Kong Bundy could turn me around.

Similarly, I didn't pay much attention as the faces of
Steve Austin and the Rock were seen on the black t-shirts of
America's acne-faced youth throughout the '90s. Moreover, I

couldn't even bother to send flowers after learning that
Andre the Giant had been fatally dropkicked by heart failure
in 1993. Until this morning, pro wrestling fandom had been
a long-buried facet of my life.

I accidentally started thinking about wrestling on my
way in to work. I was listening to "Rumble" by Link Wray,
and my brain somehow segued to "Missing Link Wray."
From there, I thought about deceased wrestling curio the
Missing Link.

Then I wondered how many different combinations of
classic rock stars and classic wrestlers I could come up with.
This is, unfortunately, how my mind works. I took to
Twitter, and my first round looked like this:

Classic wrestling merged with classic rock: Roddy Piper at
the Gates of Dawn

Classic wrestling merged with classic rock: Nikolai Volkoff
Broadway

Classic wrestling merged with classic rock: Bob Harley Race
and the Wailers

Classic wrestling merged with classic rock: Brett "Hitman"
Heart

And it kept going from there:
Bruno Sammartina Turner

Ken Pantera
WaWho McDaniel
Sting (get it?)

Whenever I launch into goofy wordplay games like this, I'm almost immediately humbled by my friends, who are way cleverer than I. My friends Justin, Justin, and Chris were responsible for the following:

Hacksaw Jim Morrison
Dusty Springfield Rhodes
Argent Slaughter
Jake "Whitesnake" Roberts
Jimmy "Supertramp" Snuka
Stone Cold Steve Boston

Extra credit goes to my friend Dan for serving up Andre They Might Be Giants.

Stretching out from classic rock to make things more contemporary, I added:

Captain Lou Barlow
Nickel Backwinkel

Though today's flurry of "rock and wrestling" activity hasn't exactly driven me to the Allstate to see a modern-day WWE card, I'm now interested in doing some "Whatever Happened to ..." searches for the AWA stars of yesteryear.

I'm going to Irish Whip Google into a clothesline over my newfound, nostalgia-fueled, thirst for knowledge.

That thirst for knowledge led me to buy a book I simply couldn't put down: Sex, Lies, and Headlocks: The Real Story of Vince McMahon and the World Wrestling Federation, *by Shaun Assael. It's a well-written, can't put it down, document of the business of wrestling, including the demise of WWF(E) competitors like the AWA, the Ted Turner/Vince McMahon war, and the national headline-grabbing steroid allegations of the early 90s.*

Though not related in any way to music (the theme of this book), I thought I'd add this wordplay piece.

(April 15, 2010)

<u>Now Playing at the Adult Cineplex</u>

I love porn movie titles; the perfect combination of wordplay, humor, and lasciviousness.

To that end, I offer the following titles, which are as timely as a trip to your local Kerasotes:

The Back-that-ass-up Plan

Boy Story 3

Gash of the Titans

Hot Tongue Time Machine

How to Pull a Train on Your Dragon

Iron Man-Man Action 2

I'm serious ... wordplay is a compulsive exercise for me. As I was editing this manuscript for final production, I had to add the following:

(May 7, 2011)

<u>Spring and Summer Movies, 2011</u>

Dylan Dong: Head of Might

Mr. Popper's Penis

Pirates of the Caribbean: On a Stranger's Tits

Transformers: Dork in the Poon

XXX-Men: First Ass

RECKONING R.E.M.'s CATALOG

CHAPTER TEN

When I learned that R.E.M. was going to release a new album in Spring, 2011, I dismissively rolled my eyes. I'd already conditioned myself to not care about the band any more, having been frequently burned by them since the early 1990s.

Then I thought for a second: "I used to love R.E.M., it doesn't seem right to dismiss them altogether." I decided that my attitude was too extreme, and that R.E.M. deserved better. My solution was to force myself to listen to every one of their studio albums, from start to finish, in chronological order.

Here are the results:

(December 28, 2010)

Murmur

R.E.M. will release their 15th studio album, *Collapse Into Now*, in March, 2011.

Announcements from the R.E.M. camp are generally met with "ho-hum" indifference these days. I'm old enough to remember a time when a new R.E.M. album was an event, one that promised obtuse lyrics to scrutinize and Peter Buck riffs to learn.

The "event" R.E.M. from my youth didn't make it too far into the 90s. The excitement behind the band was almost at an end with the release of *Monster* (1994), and certainly a thing of the past when *New Adventures in Hi-Fi* came out in 1996. I fell in that general range; my interest started to wane during the *Out of Time* era (1991) and was completely gone once I heard *Up* all the way through (1998).

With a new R.E.M. album approaching, I decided to take inventory of the band's catalog, one disc at a time. My goal for this exercise is to take a fresh, objective look at each full-length studio disc. I want to see if albums like *Murmur* and *Reckoning* remain sacred cows. I need to see if the critics who "took back" their initial praise for *Monster* were dicks for doing so. I want to confirm whether 21st Century discs *Reveal* and *Around the Sun* are as awful as I remember them to be.

My "Retroviews" will follow the same format:

Score

Each album will be rated on a scale of 1-10. To get to my final number, I'll assign a 1-10 score to each song, based on two simple pieces of criteria: "Overall Impression" and "Will I Want to Listen to this Song Five Years from Now?

"Overall Impression" will count for a maximum of 8 points; "Will I Want to Listen ... " will count for a maximum of 2 points.

An album's overall score will be the average of all song ratings. My theory is that this will eliminate the potential for additional subjectivity, and allow for a more clinical comparison of all the band's albums.

Summary

Brief, gut reaction, thoughts on the album, free from rock critic words like "aesthetic," "craftsmanship," and "raw."

And now ... my first R.E.M. "Retroview."

R.E.M. *Murmur*
Released in 1983
Radio Free Europe (9)
Pilgrimage (7)
Laughing (4)
Talk About the Passion (10)
Moral Kiosk (6)
Perfect Circle (4)
Catapult (8)
Sitting Still (6)

9-9 (5)

Shaking Through (5)

We Walk (4)

West of the Fields (5)

Overall score: 6.08

Summary:

R.E.M.'s, jangly, spirited, first full-length has been considered untouchable for decades now.

When *Murmur* was first released, it was easy to forgive the album's lesser songs (mostly consigned to "Side Two"), in light of how inventive the album sounded when compared to big 1983 records like Men at Work's *Cargo* and *Colour By Numbers* by Culture Club.

The (incredible) high points of *Murmur*, "Catapult" and "Radio Free Europe" among them, in many ways wash over and forgive the album's stinkers. Taken individually, though, a song like "We Walk" sounds tossed-off and out of place. Listened to with fresh ears, "We Walk" plays like a bad Doors song written by Ringo Starr.

I've read plenty of criticism and analysis of *Murmur* over the years, much of it pointing to the "timeless" sound of its songs. If I had to pick one "timeless" song on the album, I'd go with "Talk About the Passion," a song that can stop me dead in my tracks whenever I hear it. "Passion" is unquestionably one of Peter Buck's signature guitar songs, and one of Michael Stipe's more, well, passionate vocal performances.

Not quite the "must own" I remember it to be, but an incredible debut album nonetheless. The good songs on *Murmur* aren't merely good, they're great.

(December 29, 2010)

R.E.M. *Reckoning*

R.E.M. *Reckoning*

Released in 1984

Harborcoat (7)

7 Chinese Bros. (8)

So. Central Rain (I'm Sorry) (10)

Pretty Persuasion (9)

Time After Time (AnnElise) (7)

Second Guessing (6)

Letter Never Sent (5)

Camera (6)

(Don't Go Back to) Rockville (8)

Little America (7)

Overall score: 7.3

Summary:

Satisfying and consistent. As good as I'd remembered. "Time After Time" was a nice surprise to come back to. I'd never before realized how Velvet-y it sounds. "So. Central Rain," "Rockville," and "7 Chinese Brothers" are perfect.

(December 29, 2010)

R.E.M. *Fables of the Reconstruction*

R.E.M. *Fables of the Reconstruction*

Released in 1985

Feeling Gravitys Pull (7)

Maps and Legends (7)

Driver 8 (9)

Life and How to Live It (5)

Old Man Kensey (4)

Can't Get There From Here (6)

Green Grow the Rushes (5)

Kohoutek (5)

Auctioneer (Another Engine) (5)

Good Advices (5)

Wendell Gee (4)

Overall Score: 5.64

Summary:

The first three songs tricked me into thinking that "Fables" is a classic. In actuality, the album plays in the same way that a 15-1 horse runs. It starts strong out of the gate, and then quickly shows signs of fading before eventually dropping out completely.

"Can't Get There From Here" is one of the R.E.M. songs from my childhood that I've long held in high regard. After listening again today, it sadly doesn't hold up. "Driver 8," however, has greatly improved with age.

(December 30, 2010)

R.E.M. *Life's Rich Pageant*

R.E.M. *Life's Rich Pageant*

Released in 1986

Begin The Begin (8)

These Days (6)

Fall On Me (7)

Cuyahoga (7)

Hyena (6)

Underneath The Bunker (3)

The Flowers Of Guatemala (4)

I Believe (5)

What If We Give It Away? (8)

Just A Touch (6)

Swan Swan H (6)

Superman (7)

Overall Score: 6.08

Summary:

    "Begin the Begin" serves as a blockbuster opener (that riff; oh god, that riff) to an album that, in its consistency, is more akin to *Reckoning*.

    Stipe's voice is more clear on *Life's Rich Pageant*, though the message behind the lyrics remains muddy, if not confounding. And, sure, that's part of the charm.

(December 30, 2010)

R.E.M. *Document*

R.E.M. *Document*

Released in 1987

Finest Worksong (8)

Welcome to the Occupation (6)

Exhuming McCarthy (10)

Disturbance at the Heron House (7)

Strange (7)

It's the End of the World (8)

The One I Love (10)

Fireplace (5)

Lightnin' Hopkins (4)

King of Birds (5)

Oddfellows Local 151 (7)

Overall Score: 7.0

Summary:

When *Document* was released, the cool kids' secret had slipped out: every dipshit in America was talking about R.E.M.

Document gave the world (at least for a little while) a tougher-sounding R.E.M., a band unafraid to experiment and take chances. Without any transparent artistic compromise, they managed to deliver a game-changing, platinum, "hit" record. Consider the band's first Top 10 single, "The One I Love." The few lyrics that do exist are totally dark, e.g. "A simple prop to occupy my time/This one goes out to the one I love."

Listening to *Document* fresh today, I completely fell in love with the garage band bashery, simple riffs, and "doo doos" on "Strange." One of many pleasures on a highly recommended album.

As a final note: referring back to the rating system I established with Murmur, I assign a maximum of two points based on the criteria, "Will I Want to Listen to This Song Five Years From Now?" I gave "It's the End of the World" a "0" out of the maximum 2 points--although it's a great song, it's simply one that I never, ever, want to hear again.

(December 31, 2010)

R.E.M. *Green*

R.E.M. *Green*

Released in 1988

Pop Song 89 (7)

Get Up (8)

You Are The Everything (2)

Stand (5)

World Leader Pretend (5)

The Wrong Child (5)

Orange Crush (9)

Turn You Inside-Out (7)

Hairshirt (5)

I Remember California (3)

Untitled (3)

Overall Score: 5.37

Summary:

The mandolin. Fuck. Me. Running. This is the R.E.M. album where the instrument reared its ugly head, making me enjoy an otherwise-okay ballad like "Hairshirt" a little bit less.

Green is an all-over-the-place mess, the album sounding like R.E.M. decided to record a 40-minute argument about which creative direction they should go in.

"World Leader Pretend" is considered a monumental song in the R.E.M. oeuvre for reasons I can't understand.

Considering the brighter, cleaner production on *Green*, the song (really more of a dirge) lays bare Michael Stipe's deficits as a singer. He's got a charismatic voice ... an expressive voice ... just not a terribly strong singing voice.

Rip "Orange Crush" and "Get Up" to your hard drive and move on.

(December 31, 2010)

R.E.M. *Out of Time*

R.E.M. *Out of Time*

Released in 1991

Radio Song (4)

Losing My Religion (5)

Low (5)

Near Wild Heaven (2)

Endgame (3)

Shiny Happy People (1)

Belong (4)

Half A World Away (6)

Texarkana (7)

Country Feedback (5)

Me In Honey (8)

Overall score: 4.55

Summary:

To quote "Radio Song": "The world is collapsing around our ears." Everything I thought and held dear about R.E.M. in the 1980s gets blown up on *Out of Time*.

Out of Time is the first R.E.M. album that took more than a year to release, and perhaps it's coincidental, but the songs sound completely overdone and overthought.

"Radio Song" is awkward and embarrassing to hear with modern ears. Once you get past that song and the mandolin-driven "Religion," you land on "Low," a limp, trying, drag on the human spirit. "Endgame" is a struggling, almost-instrumental that brings *Out of Time* to a desperate halt immediately before the up-with-people pop drippery that is "Shiny Happy People." Speaking of which, "Shiny Happy People" is so sugar-sweet, I gain weight every time I listen to it.

Guest vocalist Kate Pierson, heard on "Shiny," also has a turn on "Me In Honey." Interestingly, the two Pierson songs represent the highest and lowest points on the album. The points in between are barely worth mentioning.

(January 6, 2011)

R.E.M. *Automatic for the People*

R.E.M. *Automatic for the People*

Released in 1992

Drive-8

Try Not to Breathe-6

The Sidewinder Sleeps Tonite-6

Everybody Hurts-5

New Orleans Instrumental-1

Sweetness Follows-5

Monty Got a Raw Deal-7

Ignoreland-7

Star Me Kitten-4

Man on the Moon-7

Nightswimming-3

Find the River-3

Overall Score: 5.17

Summary:

Out of Time part two. Only this time around, it's better

R.E.M. used to blast out of the gate with hold-on-to-your-seat, holy shit, barnburning opening tracks. "Drive" isn't any of those, though its moody and hypnotic sense of desolation works just as well in setting a tone.

I spent most of the past 20 years thinking I hate this album. There are certainly songs I don't like at all, including

"Everybody Hurts" and "Nightswimming," but the album's
not *that* bad.

(January 7, 2011)

R.E.M. *Monster*

R.E.M. *Monster*

Released in 1994

What's the Frequency, Kenneth?-6

Crush With Eyeliner-7

King of Comedy-4

I Don't Sleep, I Dream-8

Star 69-4

Strange Currencies-5

Tongue-1

Band and Blame-8

I Took Your Name-6

Let Me In-5

Circus Envy-8

You-4

Overall Score: 5.5

Summary:

Monster is Peter Buck's album, its edges punched into pulp by Buck's riffery and body drenched in waves of glorious feedback.

Coming off of *Automatic for the People* and *Out of Time*, the noise and racket are both welcome and reassuring. The opening, ground-splitting, vibrations of "Crush With Eyeliner" make it clear that R.E.M. hasn't forgotten how to actually, you know, *rock*.

"Circus Envy," buried at the end of *Monster*, is "classic" R.E.M., a song that holds up to anything they did in the 1980s. Stipe's lyrics are one of the album's real disappointments, especially on "Star 69" ("I know you called, I know you called, I know you hung up my line") and "King of Comedy" ("Make your money with a suit and tie"/"Make your money with shrewd denial"). Perhaps it was better when we couldn't actually understand what he was saying. The converse to those songs is "Let Me In," an affecting (and again, feedbacky), song about Kurt Cobain.

Another disappointment is a song that brings the entire album down: "Tongue." No one ever needs to hear Michael Stipe sing falsetto.

(January 8, 2011)

R.E.M. *New Adventures in Hi-Fi*

R.E.M. *New Adventures in Hi-Fi*

Released in 1996

1. How the West Was Won-7
2. The Wake-Up Bomb-6
3. New Test Leper-4
4. Undertow-7
5. E-Bow the Letter-7
6. Leave-10
7. Departure-7
8. Bittersweet Me-6
9. Be Mine-6
10. Binky the Doormat-6
11. Zither-3
12. So Fast, So Numb-7
13. Low Desert-5
14. Electrolite--5

Total Score: 6.14

Summary:

I remember really liking *New Adventures in Hi-Fi* when it first came out.

Since it's been, oh, 14 years since I last took the time to listen to "Hi-Fi" in its entirety, I assumed that my memories of the album's goodness were inflated. As I listened this time around, I made sure to cast album assumptions, recollections, and beliefs aside, essentially turning myself into an R.E.M. Tabula rasa.

Over the past two days, I listened to "Hi-Fi" three times through. With that dedicated effort behind me, I feel wholly confident in saying that it's R.E.M.'s best album of the 1990s.

When *New Adventures in Hi-Fi* first came out, the band practically removed themselves from alt-rock contention and buzzworthiness by releasing the spooky and desperate-sounding, Patti Smith-backed, "E-Bow the Letter" as its first single. Lyrically, the track seems to cover two sources of angst typical of a band whose most culturally impactful days were coming up in the rearview: fame and aging. "E-Bow" was good when I first heard it, but after reintroducing myself to the song, I'm left positively haunted by it. And no, I don't know what this means: "Aluminum, it tastes like fear/Adrenaline, it pulls us near," but Stipe's lyrics are best when they're quotably obtuse.

"I lost myself in sorrow, I lost myself in pain, I lost myself in clarity."

I can't talk about this album without singling out the most unjustly ignored song in R.E.M.'s catalog, "Leave." After a delicate instrumental lead-in, "Leave" spirals out of the speakers, driven along by a looped siren/feedback wail. Layered in sound textures, "Leave" is an arresting epic, one that takes inventory of each creative direction the band had taken prior to "Hi-Fi."

"Hi-Fi" is a great, undervalued album. It makes *Monster* seem like a warm-up and *Out of Time* seem like a painful misstep.

Coming off this exceptional release, I'm positively dreading having to listen to the next few R.E.M. albums. Dreading. It.

(January 9, 2011)

R.E.M. *Up*

R.E.M. *Up*

Released in 1998

1. Airportman-2
2. Lotus-4
3. Suspicion-3
4. Hope-4
5. At My Most Beautiful-1
6. The Apologist-2
7. Sad Professor-2
8. You're in the Air-1
9. Walk Unafraid-5
10. Why Not Smile-1
11. Daysleeper-4
12. Diminished / I'm Not Over You-2
13. Parakeet-1
14. Falls to Climb-5

Overall score: 2.64

Summary:

The less said, the better. This album is to R.E.M. what waterboarding is to U.S. foreign relations.

No Bill Berry. No teeth. No joy. No, I'll never listen to it again.

(January 14, 2011)

R.E.M. *Reveal*

R.E.M. *Reveal*

Released in 2001

1. The Lifting-5
2. I've Been High-4
3. All the Way to Reno (You're Gonna Be a Star)-5
4. She Just Wants to Be-6
5. Disappear-4
6. Saturn Return-4
7. Beat a Drum-4
8. Imitation of Life-6
9. Summer Turns to High-2
10. Chorus and the Ring-4
11. I'll Take the Rain-4
12. Beachball-1

Total score: 4.08

Summary:

For a fleeting moment in 2001, I was the Music Director of WXRT. It was a brief career stopover, and something scarcely worth noting in the ongoing history of that legendary radio station, but I was there.

I remember the day the station got advance copies of *Reveal*. The Program Director suggested we both take the album home and take a good, hard listen to determine which songs were the most "airplay worthy."

"None of them," I said the next morning. "The album's a total buzzkill and the band sounds lost." It wasn't a popular answer. I then followed up with my "least worst" choices: "She Just Wants to Be" and "The Lifting" ("Imitation of Life" was as good as those, but already getting airtime). Credit to XRT: they'll stick by and support an artist even when they shit out a turd like *Reveal*.

I wondered if my feelings would change when I returned to the album almost 10 years later.

Nope.

It's a much better album than *Up*, at least.

(January 14, 2011)

R.E.M. *Around the Sun*

R.E.M. *Around the Sun*

Released in 2004

1. Leaving New York-4
2. Electric Blue-3
3. The Outsiders-3
4. Make it All Okay-4
5. Final Straw-5
6. I Wanted to Be Wrong-3
7. Wanderlust-3
8. Boy in the Well-4
9. Aftermath-4
10. High Speed Train-2
11. The Worst Joke Ever-3
12. The Ascent of Man-1
13. Around the Sun-4

Total Score: 3.31

Summary:

Insert your own worst joke ever about this album being R.E.M.'s "Worst Joke Ever."

In my *Reveal* commentary, I said that R.E.M. sounded "lost." On *Around the Sun*, they've surpassed "lost;" they're left for dead. It's an elementary observation, but the more time that passed without percussive backbone Bill Berry behind them, the less capable R.E.M. became of creating meaningful, evocative music.

To be sure, *Around the Sun* is bland melancholia. With dopier lyrics than usual, too:

I jump on a high speed train
I'll never look back again
I flail like the antelope
Who jumped from the building

What does it mean? It means "fuck you, citizen."

(January 14, 2011)

R.E.M. *Accelerate*

R.E.M. *Accelerate*

Released in 2008

1. Living Well is the Best Revenge-9

2. Man-Sized Wreath-7

3. Supernatural Superserious-6

4. Hollow Man-5

5. Houston-5

6. Accelerate-6

7. Until the Day is Done-4

8. Mr. Richards-3

9. Sing for the Submarine-5

10. Horse to Water-5

11. I'm Gonna DJ-1

Total score: 5.09

Summary:

They live.

The first three songs on *Accelerate* are as convincing an argument as you'll find for post-90s R.E.M. Case in point: "Living Well is the Best Revenge," which is far and away the best R.E.M. song since the release of *New Adventures in Hi-Fi* in '96.

While *Accelerate* is a welcome relief from the watered- and broken-down band responsible for the previous three albums, there are still moments where R.E.M. misses the mark. The lyrics of "I'm Gonna DJ" reveal an aging Michael Stipe striving for relevance, spitting out lines like "If death is pretty final/I'm collecting vinyl/I'm gonna DJ at the end of the world."

Most all's forgiven, though. *Accelerate* marks the moment when R.E.M. remembered how to rock.

(January 14, 2011)

The Best of R.E.M.: The Results Ranked!

Less than a month ago, I started on a mission to reacquaint myself with every song and album in R.E.M.'s studio discography. Earlier tonight, I finished that exercise with a "retroview" of *Accelerate*.

Now that the heavy lifting's finished, I can format my efforts into something meaningful.

As a reminder, here's how I judged every song and album:

Each album will be rated on a scale of 1-10. To get to my final number, I'll assign a 1-10 score to each song, based on two simple pieces of criteria: "Overall Impression" and "Will I Want to Listen to this Song Five Years from Now?"

"Overall Impression" will count for a maximum of 8 points; "Will I Want to Listen ..." will count for a maximum of 2 points.

An album's overall score will be the average of all song ratings. My theory is that this will eliminate the potential for additional subjectivity, and allow for a more clinical comparison of all the band's albums.

Using the results of my R.E.M. exercise, I've ranked, with confidence, the R.E.M. discography from best to worst, including each album's overall score:

1. *Reckoning* (7.30)
2. *Document* (7.0)
3. *New Adventures in Hi-Fi* (6.14)

4. *Murmur* (6.08)

4. *Life's Rich Pageant* (6.08)

6. *Fables of the Reconstruction* (5.64)

7. *Monster* (5.5)

8. *Green* (5.37)

9. *Automatic for the People* (5.17)

10. *Accelerate* (5.09)

11. *Out of Time* (4.55)

12. *Reveal* (4.08)

13. *Around the Sun* (3.31)

14. *Up* (2.64)

If you want to build an R.E.M. library a la carte, here are the 20 songs that ranked between 8-10:

<u>10</u>

Exhuming McCarthy

Leave

So. Central Rain

The One I Love

<u>9</u>

Driver 8

Living Well is the Best Revenge

Orange Crush

Pretty Persausion

Radio Free Europe

<u>8</u>

(Don't Go Back to) Rockville

Begin the Begin

Bang and Blame

Catapult

Circus Envy

Drive

Finest Worksong

Get Up

I Don't Sleep, I Dream

Me in Honey

What if We Give it Away

FROM THE OUTSIDE: ALICE COOPER

CHAPTER ELEVEN

How it took until 2011 to get Alice inducted into the Rock and Roll Hall of Fame is a mystery to me.

I've been an Alice Cooper fan since I saw him perform "School's Out" on the Muppet Show *in the 70s. Less than a year after his Muppets appearance, I vividly remember going with my grandmother to the corner newsstand on Main and Chicago, in Evanston, to buy a copy of* Marvel Premiere #50, *a comic book adaptation of Alice's asylum-themed* From the Inside *album.*

The Alice Cooper library includes a wealth of songs. Narrowing them down to essentials is almost impossible, though I tried a few years back:

(Tuesday, January 18, 2005)

<u>Alice Cooper Mix CD</u>

I've been revisiting and rethinking the Alice Cooper library over the past few days. The result? A pretty solid mix CD, which I hastily compiled before work, and listened to on my way in:

1. "Generation Landslide"
2. "Who Do You Think We Are?"
3. "Desperado"
4. "Ballad of Dwight Fry"
5. "Clones"
6. "Serious"
7. "Billion Dollar Babies"
8. "Cold Ethyl"
9. "Pain"
10. "Public Animal #9"
11. "Inmates"
12. "Disgraceland"
13. "Is It My Body?"

Music journalism is a very difficult thing to master, and only a few working critics actually do an exemplary job of it.

Chicago can proudly lay claim to two of the best rock journalists working today: Jim DeRogatis and Greg Kot. Their work, be it books they've published (e.g. Let it Blurt, by DeRogatis, and Ripped, by Kot) or daily blog entries, is as good as rock journalism gets. I can't play in their sandbox, let alone in the same park.

I've never had any ambitions to be a music write.. However, when my friend Patrick asked me to review a new Alice Cooper album for his metal e-zine (Detritus), I couldn't say "no."

Along Came A Spider (*CD review originally written for* Detritus, 2008)

Alice Cooper

Along Came a Spider

(SPV)

A new Alice Cooper album really only exists to serve existing Alice Cooper fans, and those fans are getting harder to please. Most gave up after *Trash,* and those still on board have only grudgingly accepted later-in-life releases like *The Last Temptation* and *The Eyes of Alice Cooper.* Call it a sense of duty. Call it nostalgia. Call it an unfulfillable hope that somehow Alice will write another song like "Elected" or "Ballad of Dwight Fry" before he goes to the Great Back Nine in the sky.

Because the possible appeal and saturation level of an Alice Cooper album in 2008 is limited to the black-mascaraed faithful, the only way to look at his recent concept album about serial killing, *Along Came a Spider*, is to hold it up against his previous four decades of catalog.

First, the good: *Along Came a Spider* has a more well-expressed concept than Alice's watershed entry into the concept album arena, *Welcome to My Nightmare*. In a reverent nod, that album's Steven manages to scare up a reference before ACaS's boo-scary, plot-twist closing.

Along Came a Spider tells the James Patterson-lite story of a serial killer who creates a spider from the parts of his victims (those victims are wrapped in silk, 'natch). It's over-the-top, ridiculous—even stupid, at times. It's also as close to "classic," theatrical Alice as we've seen in a long while.

The best songs on the album, two in sum, are as good or better than anything since the late-80s. "(In Touch With) Your Feminine Side" is instantly familiar, seemingly crafted for fist-pumping karaoke sessions in either the violent crimes wing of your local prison or one of the outer rings of hell. Lyrically, it could be taken as an AC/DC-penned, lusty obsession for a member of the opposite sex. Looking at it within the album's greater context, it's really just a creepy ode to calculated stalking.

Stronger still is the soaring anthem "Salvation," with its melancholy contemplation and pianos giving way to crashing guitars, understated guitar solo, and commanding vocal performance. It's "Spider's" finest moment; one that would have sounded just as natural on Cooper's semi-autobiographical (and entirely underrated) insane asylum chronicle, *From the Inside*.

Moving beyond "Salvation" and "Feminine Side," the songs on *Along Came a Spider* are merely okay—not awful when they pop up in an iPod Shuffle, but nothing to intentionally add to an iPod playlist. The album's "single," "Vengeance Is Mine," is mostly aimless, though ultimately harmless. And so goes the rest of the disc.

Looking at the album as one body of work, where the sum of the parts is ignored for an analysis of the greater whole, "Spider" lacks real bite. For an album about a truly lunatic serial killer, a self-described "arachnophobic psychopath" ("Catch Me If You Can"), "Spider" never feels dangerous. The album's first song, "I Know Where You Live," opens with a news report that sets up the album's narrative. It's flat exposition for its own sake, and amateur-sounding at that. For true opening chills, Cooper need only refer back to the title track of his *Dada* album, which still manages to evoke spontaneous pantshittings from the faint of heart.

Since Alice Cooper's glory days, he's found his golf swing and Jesus, but has never lost his unique skew on the world and what collectively freaks us out. And while *Along Came a Spider* doesn't necessarily add to Cooper's legacy, it doesn't take away from it, either.

Finally, how does *Along Come a Spider* place among Alice's other 25 decades-spanning works?

Billion Dollar Babies >Love it to Death>Welcome to My Nightmare >From the Inside>Lace and Whiskey>Trash>School's Out>Hey Stoopid>Killer>Goes to Hell >Constrictor>Muscle of Love>Raise Your Fist and Yell>The Last Temptation>Along Came A Spider > Flush the Fashion>Dragontown>Dirty Diamonds>Easy Action >Brutal Planet> Dada>The Eyes of Alice Cooper>Special Forces>Pretties for You>Zipper Catches Skin

I've seen Alice perform twice in the 21ˢᵗ Century, at decidedly inauspicious venues: The Star Plaza (Merrillville, IN) and Genesee (Waukegan, IL).

Spontaneity isn't much of a factor at Alice shows; his setlist is almost always the same. Fans are treated to a "greatest hits," Vegas-style, song package that may include one or two recent songs. The unchanging, predictable, run-through of his hits would be shameful if Alice wasn't as good as he (still) is.

(August 30, 2008)

Alice Cooper in Waukegan: Review

Alice Cooper slayed (find me a verb more appropriate, I dare you) last night. The show punched my face clean off and then poured rubbing alcohol on whatever pulp was left.

Alice Cooper has taken up a proud tradition former legends have been successfully employing for years: using young, mostly-anonymous, and hungry players to make the live show seem vital and not like a sad stab at recreating the so-called "glory years."

That doesn't mean the glory years weren't revisited. The concert was essentially divided into two sets, the first of which was a raw, club-level, rendering of Cooper's greatest hits. Library essentials like "Eighteen," "No More Mr. Nice Guy," "Is It My Body" and even the (relatively) more modern "Feed My Frankenstein" and "Lost in America" were ripped through with a toughness and sense of rock and roll danger I had (wrongly) assumed Alice Cooper was long past creating in his sixth decade of life and fourth decade of live performance.

The band jumped from song to song without any insulting stage patter or time to allow the audience to catch its breath. There was no, "Thank you Chicago, how ya feeling tonight;" no "Anyone here eighteen years old? Well, this song's for you!" After the first four songs had completely kicked my ass, I leaned over to my friend Patrick to say, "This show is absolutely his to fuck up." I've seen too many concerts where, just as things were going in the right direction, the entire experience was sabotaged by either substandard new material, cheesy banter, or by-the-number and/or bored recitations of older songs. None of that happened. There were only two new songs played last night--that's it. And they weren't half-bad.

There is no presence on stage like Alice Cooper, no frontman as commanding. Cooper prowls the stage like he's surveying an army of his own malevolent creation, taunting the audience while twirling objects ranging from cane to riding crop to sword, spinning each with Three Musketeers precision. With his make-up on, masterful stage persona, and the fountain of youth all-stars backing him up, I never once felt like I was watching on old man past his prime. Instead, I was watching Alice Cooper, superstar. Just as it was supposed to be.

The second set was devoted to pure Cooper theatrics, the sort of thing that helped elevate him to stadium-filling status in the 70s. A handful of tracks from *Welcome to My*

Nightmare, the chilling "Steven" among them, played out as an on-stage plunge into insanity, complete with straightjacket and enraged version of "The Ballad of Dwight Fry" to cap it off. The bit concluded not with a beheading (okay, kind of a disappointment), but a hanging (still a good time).

By the time I got to the first song of the encore, "Billion Dollar Babies," I'd had the time of my life. I walked into the venue not knowing what to expect and walked out feeling like I'd seen the show of the year.

LISTS

CHAPTER TWELVE

People love lists, especially when they're applied to the world of entertainment. I'm one of those people (in fact, let me tell you all the reasons why …).

As a long-time comic book reader, drawing a line between certain superheroes and heavy metal seemed like a totally natural thing to do.

(April 25, 2009)

The Top 5 Most Metal Superheroes Ever

At its most bombastic (and in some cases, most interesting), heavy metal can sound like an audiobook

version of a comic book. You can almost see a Marvel or
D.C. logo printed on songs about warriors waving
broadswords at legions of undead, visits to the flaming pits
of hell, or late night extraterrestrial visitations.

Furthering the case for the metal and comics symbiosis, I
offer up a list of the TOP 5 MOST METAL SUPERHEROES
EVER:

1. Thor. He's the freaking Norse God of Thunder, which
means that Vikings worshipped him. And honestly, what
could be more metal than making your mark with a storm-
creating hammer? The Asgardian, as imagined by Stan Lee
and Jack Kirby, even has the same hair that David Lee Roth
had when Van Halen recorded "I'm the One." There's even a
metal artist who's assumed Thor's identity. The son of Odin
is a total (golden) lock for #1.

2. Doctor Strange. He utters arcane mystic incantations.
He hangs out in a secret man cave in the heart of Greenwich
Village and dates a goth chick with white hair. He has a
rogues gallery that includes some of hell's A-listers and
ETERNITY. That's all of eternity, mind you. That's not just
metal, that's completely badass.

3. The Spectre. The embodiment of the wrath of God,
this spook does all of the big guy's wetwork. The Spectre has
been known to melt and torture evildoers. His skin is also
completely pale, like he's been holed up in a basement
listening to Venom records and playing World of Warcraft
for the past five years straight.

4. Iron Fist. He learned Kung fu in a secret city and earned his chest tattoo by stealing it off a giant scar on a dragon's chest. Because he can turn his fist into something iron-like, he's registered as a lethal weapon with the government. Kung fu, dragons, and deadly power are metal enough for this Hero for Hire to make the Top 5.

5. Jonah Hex. The disfigured hero from D.C.'s version of the Wild West is the typical comics antihero (see also: Wolverine, John Constantine, Deadpool, and Ghost Rider-- metal heroes, one and all). Jonah kills people for money, while serving a higher sense of frontier justice. Liquor, guns, and whorehouses define Hex's world, not unlike the world of Pantera in the 90s.

Why stop there?

(April 26, 2009)

More of the Most Metal Superheroes Ever

1. Daimon Hellstorm. My friend Patrick--the most metal guy I know, was quick to point out this no-brainer. He wrote in an email today, "Huge pentagram tattoo, can summon Hellfire, and has the most metal aspect ever--his Dad's the Devil!"

2. Green Arrow. Green Arrow doesn't fight crime. He bowhunts it.

3. Zatanna. Round One of this idea left me with a toss-up between Zatanna and fellow sorcerer Doctor Strange. Zatanna gets metal credit for looking like a Suicide Girl, her

mastery of magic, and for having the stones to mindwipe Batman. Most superheroes don't have the courage to even look Batman in the eye; old girl done stole his memory.

4. Iron Man. There's a Black Sabbath song of the same name (that admittedly has nothing to do with the Avenger). Beyond that, though, Tony Stark has never met a cocktail, party, or cocktail party he didn't like. Party on, Shellhead.

5. Etrigan the Demon. He's on a first-name basis with Merlin and has fought Morgaine le Fay. Take that, Kamelot! He's also lived for centuries bonded to a man whose last name is Blood, which reminds me of the Hammerfall song "Blood Bound."

Here's an article from 2005 that was rejected for a book of rock lists that, to my knowledge, never materialized:

Atlas Hugged

By James VanOsdol

The names of cities and landmarks have always been fair game in rock and roll nomenclature. Here are some of our favorite Mapquest-friendly bands:

Alter Bridge

Alter Bridge, essentially the "classic" Creed line-up with a new lead singer, debuted in August, 2004—just months after the official press release of Creed's disbandment hit the music world. Starting over isn't easy, especially coming off the arena-filling, chart-topping (two #1 albums), multi-platinum hugeness of Creed. Guitarist Mark Tremonti acknowledged that by naming the new band after a bridge in his hometown of Detroit that symbolically divided the "haves" and "have nots." Alter Bridge's first album, *One Day Remains*, just barely went gold, falling way short of Creed-level heights. At press time, the band was working on a follow-up.

Boston

Boston's self-titled first album, released in 1976, reached #3 on the Billboard chart, thanks to big hit songs like "More Than a Feeling." The follow-up, "Don't Look Back," went right to #1. It's impossible for current generations to grasp just how big they were "back in the day" — their first gig in New York was headlining Madison Square Garden. The seeds for Boston (and the band's name) were planted just three miles outside of Boston city limits. Band mastermind Tom Scholz recorded the demos that would eventually become the first Boston album while working on a master's degree at M.I.T.

Soundgarden

Yes, there actually is a "sound garden." The Seattle grunge giants ("Spoonman," "Black Hole Sun," "The Day I Tried to Live") took their name from a sculpture near Seattle's Magnuson Park that makes all sorts of bizarre noises when the wind blows. After an 11-year run that included two Grammys and two Top 5 albums, Soundgarden called it quits in 1997. Singer Chris Cornell has had the most successful post-Soundgarden career, as both a solo artist and frontman of Audioslave.

MC5

Back when they started in 1964, the mainstream didn't pay much attention to this proud-to-be-from-Detroit (the "MC" stands for "Motor City") band. Since then, the MC5 (along with fellow Motor City rockers the Stooges) have been regarded as one of the architects of modern hard rock, metal, and punk. For decades running, garage bands across America have been banging out "Kick Out the Jams" as a rite of passage. More famous admirers like Rage Against the

Machine, Blue Oyster Cult, and Jeff Buckley have covered it, too.

Laibach

The only Slovenian band on the list. Probably the only Slovenian band to get attention in America, for that matter. For their name, the bleak, experimental, and controversial band took on the title given to the city of Ljubljana by the Germans during World War II. Throughout their career, which started in the early '80s and continues today, the politically-charged Laibach has resisted acknowledging individuals in the group, preferring only to discuss "the collective." Well-known for their covers, Laibach's reworking of the Beatles' *Let it Be* album (everything except the title track) is a disturbing, dramatic, industrial, almost operatic, affair.

Cypress Hill

The lazy, pro-marijuana ("Hits from the Bong" being the first of many dead giveaways) rap of Cypress Hill got its start in South Central L.A., whose Cypress Street was the inspiration for the group's name. The first "superstar" Latino rap group, Cypress Hill (B-Real, Sen Dog, Muggs) forced the world to take notice by going straight to number one with their second album, *Black Sunday*, in 1993. Cypress Hill has courted rock audiences throughout their career, playing decidedly non-rap festivals like Lollapalooza ('92, '94, '95) and Woodstock '94.

Starting back in 1992, I spent my Decembers obsessing over the creation of my annual "Best of" lists.

Each year, I'd sequester myself in my home office with only Nilla Wafers and Diet Coke to sustain me. I'd pass the (many/late) hours scrutinizing and reviewing the previous year in music and trying to sort the year's albums and highlights in a meaningful way.

I created those lists for just over a decade before politely excusing myself from the process in 2003. I've only created one since then, in 2006, because I felt like I "had to" as a full-time Q101 DJ.

This past year (2010), I got fed up altogether with "Best of" and "Top 10" lists. Taking a close look at what the critics and blogerati published at year's end, all I saw were resequenced versions of the same pool of shit albums, the majority of which will be forgotten in less than five years' time.

(December 13, 2010)

BEST OF 2010

I haven't done a "Top 10" or "Best of" list for years.

Looking back at previous lists, I found that some of my picks were agonizingly misguided and/or not as honest as they could've been. It's for the best that I stopped doing them.

With my own listmaking sidelined, I've been watching the "Best of 2010" lists roll in. Every one of them seems to be a slightly different version of the same 10 albums:

Kanye West *My Beautiful Dark Twisted Fantasy*

Deerhunter *Halcyon Digest*

Neil Young *Le Noise*

The National *High Violet*

Robyn *Body Talk*

Eminem *Recovery*

Grinderman *Grinderman 2*

LCD Soundsystem *This is Happening*

Arcade Fire *The Suburbs*

Sleigh Bells *Treats*

There had to be other music worth noting in 2010, right? Right?

Here are two of my lists from years past: A "Best of Everything" list from 2004, and a "Top 10" music list from 2006.

(December 20, 2004)

<u>THE BEST OF 2004</u>

2004 was a much better year for entertainment than 2003, but I've decided not do a straightforward music list. Instead, here's a list of things I liked, musical and otherwise, in 2004.

1. *Spiderman 2*

2. "Gay Robot," track from Adam Sandler's *Shhh Don't Tell*

3. Mastadon *Leviathan*

4. SOiL "Pride," lead track from *Redefine*

5. Neko Case *The Tigers Have Spoken*

6. In Flames *Soundtrack To Your Escape*

7. *Justice League Unlimited* on Cartoon Network

8. The Jack Ryan story. Sex clubs. Jeri Ryan. Fantastic.

9. The Fall *The Real New Fall LP*

10. Burrito bowl at Chipotle, just black beans, rice, and corn salsa.

11. *Dodgeball*

12. *The Incredibles*

13. *Identity Crisis* (addendum, 12/23/04-I wrote this before I read the last issue, which was a total letdown)

14. The Olympics. I can't believe I enjoyed watching them as much as I did.

15. Lindsay Lohan. Just because.

16. *The Taking* by Dean Koontz

17. *Team America*. "Freedom isn't free. There's a hefty fucking fee."

18. Rammstein "Moskau," track from *Reise Reise*

19. *24*

20. The Libertines *The Libertines*

21. "Disposable Heroes" seen and heard live at the Allstate.

22. David Cross *It's Not Funny*

23. Motorhead *Inferno*

24. Obama at the DNC

25. Dogs Die In Hot Cars "I Love You Cause I Have To," track from *Please Describe Yourself*

26. Local H "Everyone Alive," track from *Whatever Happened to P.J. Soles*

27. All signs pointing to the demise of reality TV.

28. William Shatner "Common People," track from *Has Been*. Notable for so many reasons, including the first engaging vocal performance Joe Jackson has delivered since the 1980's.

29. Slipknot *Vol. 3 (The Subliminal Verses)*

30. Monster Magnet "The Right Stuff," Hawkwind cover from *Monolithic Baby*. Lackluster album, whose main strengths were this and a David Gilmour cover.

31. Caviar *The Thin Mercury Sound*

32. "Ex-Machina" (Wildstorm)

33. *Lord of the Rings: Return of the King* (Extended DVD set)

34. *Eats, Shoots & Leaves* by Lynne Truss

35. Velvet Revolver "Do It For The Kids," track off *Contraband*

36. *The Zero Game* by Brad Meltzer

37. Nick Cave and the Bad Seeds *Abattoir Blues/The Lyre of Orpheus*

38. *Hellboy*

39. Probot (with Kurt Brecht) "Silent Spring," track from *Probot*

40. Old 97's *Drag It Up*

41. Cradle of Filth "Nymphetamine," single version

Best of 2006

I just had to do my "Best of 2006" iMix for Q101.com, so it seemed like a good time to post the albums those songs came from. Here's what I listened to most in '06:

1. Mission of Burma *The Obliterati*

2. The Hold Steady *Boys and Girls in America*

3. Rhapsody of Fire *Triumph or Agony*

4. Art Brut *Bang Bang Rock & Roll*

5. Secret Machines *Ten Silver Drops*

6. Califone *Roots and Crowns*

7. Mastodon *Blood Mountain*

8. Belle and Sebastian *The Life Pursuit*

9. The Changes *Today is Tonight*

10. Starlight Mints *Drowaton*

Ed. Notes, 2011: Yikes. I always hated Belle and Sebastian. And the Starlight Mints? Really? What a poser I was.

At the end of '07 I put together a list that that I'm not embarrassed to look at a few years later. I still listen to at least half of these albums with some regularity:

Best Metal Albums of 2007

Therion *Gothic Kabbalah*

Moonsorrow *V: Havitetty*

Witchcraft *The Alchemist*

Municipal Waste *The Art of Partying*

Fairyland *The Fall of an Empire*

Dark Tranquility *Fiction*

Symphony X *Paradise Lost*

High on Fire *Death is This Communion*

Slayer *Christ Illusion*

Nocturnal Rites *The 8th Sin*

Kamelot *Ghost Opera*

Pig Destroyer *Phantom Limb*

Machine Head *The Blackening*

I wish I had been this smart when I first started creating lists:

(December 22, 2010/Twitter)

I call BS on Top 10 lists that have "Honorable Mentions."

Make your 10 picks, stand behind them, and be done with it.

(March 12, 2007)

<u>GRUNGE MIX</u>

Every week, the Q101 D.J.'s submit custom "iMixes" to the iTunes Music Store on Q101.com. Here's a "Grunge Mix" that I just submitted:

1. 7 Year Bitch "Hip Like Junk"
2. The Gits "While You're Twisting…"
3. Nirvana "Frances Farmer …"
4. Mother Love Bone "Stardog Champion"
5. Screaming Trees "Halo of Ashes"
6. Babes in Toyland "Mother"
7. Alice in Chains "God Smack"
8. Mudhoney "Touch Me I'm Sick"
9. Hole "Violet"
10. Pearl Jam "Animal"
11. L7 "Stuck Here Again"
12. Soundgarden "Outshined"
13. Melvins "Revolve"
14. Seaweed "Card Tricks"

In hindsight, I'd probably replace "God Smack" with "Sea of Sorrow,""Halo of Ashes" with "Shadow of the Season," and "Frances Farmer…" with "On a Plain."Oh well.

(February 12, 2007)

Turning Japanese

I've recently become fascinated by, and hungry to read more of, manga. I'd pretty much ignored the genre for years, something I think a lot of 30-somethings are guilty of. And then … I picked up *Hellsing*. Then *Eden*. *Full Metal Alchemist*. A recent trip to Barnes and Noble set me back $50 in manga books alone.

With my head stuck in the land of the Rising Sun, I just submitted an iMix of Japanese music to Q101.com's iTunes Store manager. For your consideration:

Esoteric Black Hair "Are You Satisfied?"

Dir En Grey "Merciless Cult"

Guitar Wolf "Jet Generation"

Momus "I Want You, But I Don't Need You"

Kiyoshi Yoshida "The Lucky Spirit"

Pizzicato Five "It's a Beautiful Day"

Puffy AmiYumi "V-A-C-A-T-I-O-N"

Cornelius "Drop"

Shonen Knife "Riding on the Rocket"

Melt Banana "We Will Rock You"

Electric Eel Shock "Bastard!"

The Boredoms "I Am Cola"

Remember Mix CDs? I used to make 'em on a daily basis.

(June 19, 2004)

GLAM MIX

It was a "return to 70's glam" morning on my way to work. I very hurriedly this morning threw a few glam-ish songs on a CD:

Slade "Run Runaway" (80's cheese, but ...)
New York Dolls "Trash"
T. Rex "Jeepster"
Mott The Hoople "All The Way From Memphis"
Sweet "Fox On The Run"
Roxy Music "Out Of The Blue"

I couldn't bring myself to put any Gary Glitter on the disc. Had I been less concerned about rocking out to a pedophile, I would've definitely put "Do You Want to Touch Me? (Oh Yeah!)" on the disc.

(June 14, 2004)
REGGAE MIX

Awesome weather this weekend. I felt inspired by it and put together a reggae CD to listen to on my way to work today. I flashed back to many hours of misspent youth, doing rum shots as an underaged punk at Exedus on Clark.
On the CD:

Peter Tosh "Here Comes The Judge"
Willie Williams "Armagideon Time"

Dennis Brown "Westbound Train"

Black Uhuru "Leaving To Zion"

Junior Delgado "Merry-Go-Round"

Half Pint "Level The Vibes"

Desmond Dekker "007"

Burning Spear "Spear Burning" (live)

DIALED IN AND OUT: RADIO

CHAPTER THIRTEEN

*As this book heads towards its conclusion, I thought I'd go off
in a comfortable tangent: the topic of radio. Music drove me from
an early age to pursue a career in radio, and it was a love for music
that defined my on-air work on Chicago radio stations WKQX,
WZZN, and WXRT. While radio and music may not be as
obviously linked in your world, they're inextricably bonded in
mine.*

*I've always been careful about writing about radio; the idea
being that I didn't want to bite the metaphorical hand that feeds.
Program Directors (the people who hire air personalities and have
ultimate say on everything that gets aired) are notoriously tight
when it comes to managing the messages about their product.*

Perceived slights against the on-air product, parent organization, or industry traditionally have been met with a pink slip. Like I mentioned in this book's dedication: I'm a parent. My kids don't need to go hungry because their daddy wanted to say something about the station that paid his bills, or had *to make a point about the industry.*

Fear of unemployment is what I believe held the majority of Tribune Company staffers at bay as a gaggle of old-school radio guys brought the company to its knees between 2008 and 2010.

The writing was on the wall for CEO Randy Michaels and Chief Innovation Officer Lee Abrams when, on October 5, 2010, the venerable New York Times *jumped on a story Chicago media critic Robert Feder first broke in June, 2010.*

The article listed off an embarrassing scandal sheet of corporate misbehavior, describing a "bankrupt culture" that included "pervasive sex talk."

Shortly after the Times *piece ran, Abrams sent an email to the Tribune staff that (you can't make this stuff up) included links to inappropriate web content.*

(October 19, 2010)

Trials and Tribune Nation

The Tribune suspended Chief Innovation Officer Lee Abrams without pay today for his now well-discussed, inappropriate, all-staff email.

The questionable email was sent less than a week after the *New York Times* shithammered Tribune Co. for its "bankrupt culture," helmed by (groan) former radio bigwig, Randy Michaels.

The swinging dick, grabass, cowboy culture of radio is nothing new to this writer. I've weathered chains of command that couldn't even file for cultural bankruptcy. When radio showed me the door in 2007, the culture was an aspect of the business I swore I wouldn't miss. Further, I believed that it was an aspect of business that couldn't possibly exist outside of radio. Maybe it doesn't. That is, unless radio guys are brought in to run a non-radio place.

Many intelligent people whose writing and work I respect, Robert Feder (vocalo.org) and Frank Sennett (*Time Out Chicago*) among them, have raised the issue that Tribune staffers haven't made enough of a stand against the yahoos running the joint. Feder wrote today, "The timidity of so many journalists at the Tribune, WGN-Channel 9 and WGN-AM (720) to speak out makes me admire Roger Ebert even more for the way in which he took on Conrad Black and David Radler ... Or the way Carol Marin and Ron Magers confronted their NBC bosses at WMAQ-Channel 5 in the late 90s."

It's a fact that most journalists I've met hold themselves to a higher standard and fall on the knife of ethical righteousness when the cause is just. Phil Rosenthal (media columnist for the Tribune) deserves huge credit for having the stones to write about the dysfunction in his own house. Recent reports have shown that (Tribune) Editor Gerould Kern has worked to maintain the integrity and spirit of his newsroom. One has to think that Rosenthal and Kern (as well as other staffers with less public personas) put themselves at risk for calling out the Tribune Company's top brass. Radio guys are making the calls at Tribune Company. And with radio guys, dissension is the quickest way to earn a totally SFW email that "wishes you well in your future endeavors."

That said, if it were me, in this moment in time, I'd probably STFU and keep my head down if I worked for the Chicago Tribune, WGN-AM, or WGN-TV. Am I timid? A coward? Conditionally, I suppose. But I'm honest. And I know I'm not the only one in 2010 buying generic brands and wringing every last drop out of my biweekly paycheck (and putting whatever's leftover on credit). These are frightening economic times, and baby needs new shoes (or in the case of my two children, winter coats).

For someone working in any aspect of the media (e.g. print, radio, television) today, unemployment doesn't represent a temporary inconvenience; it's a promise of debilitating, core and career-shaking, destruction. Across the board, there are less jobs, less advertiser dollars coming in, and less long-term visions coming from the top. Many of the people who I shared the airwaves with in the 90s and early 00s are either out of the business completely or relocated in markets that they used to make fun of. They simply can't get back to where they once were. I have to assume a similarly bleak situation exists in the print world.

Back to Ebert, Marin, and Magers; they're giants in Chicago media. Their personalities and talents are bigger than the people managing them. They can shoulder the risk involved with making a stand when management is mismanaging and brand-damaging the organization. The rest of us? As unpopular as it is to say in the middle of the ongoing, high-minded, discussion being had about this topic, we'd rather suffer through the loss of our parent companys' principles than the loss of our homes.

Quick thoughts on radio, pulled from Twitter and my blog

(May 1, 2011)
Osama bin Laden was killed today. Unfortunately for local media, the announcement came late on a Sunday, when most radio stations are on autopilot.

I worked on the air until 9 p.m. then put the station in "auto." 30 minutes after that, news leaked of OBL's death. 8.5 hours after that, live voices returned to the air. I shudder to think how many other stations across the country were locked in the same robotic groove.

(February 26, 2011)
Listener: "Ur a really bad dj how in the fuck did you get this job." Reply:"That's rude. I would never ask you how U got your job @ Arby's."
*
(February 26, 2011)
And that was followed by another SMS requesting a song for a girl who's currently listening from an Indiana prison. JVO: #1 with criminals.
*
(February 26, 2011)
Let other radio hosts worry about coveted demographics; I've got felons on my side!
*
(February 10, 2011)

New Fresh FM billboard: "Chicago's Variety Station."
Meaningless corporate slogan. Put (AM sports talker) the
Score on that frequency & call it a day.
*

(September 20, 2010)
JACK-FM is playing Creed "Higher." They don't even have
DJs to call and swear at.
*

(May 21, 2010)
A guy named Larry the Duck just frontsold a Morrissey
song on XM. Oh, how I love wacky radio names.
*

(May 25, 2010)
Listener text: "Luvd q101 since grammer school!" Don't
know whether to celebrate the irony or just feel very, very
sad.
*

(April 10, 2010)
Just heard "Renegade" by Styx on the radio. Love the
Tommy Shaw stuff.
*

(January 9, 2009)
Clear Channel carnage: 1850 out. Breathtaking. Sobering.
*

(July 11, 2006)
I just read about a Seattle D.J. who played Weird Al's
"Amish Paradise" after the horrific schoolgirl murders in
Pennsylvania. Ha. Ha. Ha. Clever stuff.

I've always said that my "role models" for on-air delivery didn't come from radio. In fact, I probably owe more to David Letterman than I do any of Chicago's FM legends.

But when it comes to personal branding; how to define and cement an image, Bob Stroud is probably the single greatest example of career definition that I grew up listening to. He's locked himself in as an unquestioned authority on music--an enviable niche, and one I tried to emulate in my time on the air in Chicago.

We crossed paths briefly, when we both worked at WXRT for a very short time together in 2001. One of my career's great regrets is that we didn't have more of a chance to interact.

I interviewed him via email for my blog in 2009. This is an edited excerpt.

(March 17, 2009)

<u>BOB STROUD INTERVIEW</u>

Meet Bob Stroud, radio legend, whose work remains the gold standard for on-air music hosts both in and outside of Chicago.

Stroud can be heard weekdays in his role as midday host at WDRV-FM ("The Drive") and as creator and curator of the beloved long-running "Rock 'n Roll Roots" show.

<u>JVO</u>: In preparing for this interview, I thought a lot about your on-air style, which I can define in three ways: credible, super-knowledgeable, and accessible. By my recollection, you've never had to compromise your persona or how you present yourself. Am I missing any dark periods? Were

there P.D.s (Program Directors) who just "didn't get it," and asked you to do ridiculous things?

BS: Luckily, I've only worked formats that have encouraged me to be myself. Pretty much what you hear on-air is what you get off-air. And I think all of the P.D.'s I've worked for have understood that a major part of my strength is allowing me to go on air and be me. Obviously there have been "dark periods," but that didn't come with being asked to alter my presentation.

JVO: "Rock 'n Roll Roots" was one of the first specialty shows I became aware of when I was growing up. How do you keep a show like that fresh for the audience and yourself, almost three decades later?

BS: Well, in my corner is the hardcore love the audience has for the music and the era. I could probably just go on and "jukebox" the entire three hours and retain a decent-sized audience. But with that love of the music comes a wildly enthusiastic interest in the music. By that, I'm referring to everything from anecdotal stories about the songs and artists to maybe how the songs performed on the charts. That interest from both the audience and myself keeps me on the constant lookout as to how I can present the three hours with varying twists that will continue to coddle the audience into keeping "Rock 'n Roll Roots" as appointment listening.

JVO: I've heard lots of people who were too young to have actually bought records in the pre-CD era lovingly talk about the "warmth" and beauty of vinyl. While I generally don't miss the format, I think there's something to be said for the radio days before every file was digitized. Do you prefer to play your show's music from a computer, or are you ever nostalgic for the kinetic, sometimes adrenal, energy of cueing up records (or CDs)?

BS: I'm on board about the sound advantages of vinyl. I can hear it, no question. Even some of my 45's sound better than the digital domain. Yet I wouldn't go back to doing it the old school way for all the tea in China, buddy. Too much work! Modern technology allows the jock the extra added time to work through his on air rap without having to hassle with records. And quite frankly, that's what your P.D. is looking for anyway, the best on air rap you can summon up.

JVO: Let's talk about Todd Rundgren. Favorite solo album?

BS: Todd who? (Ahem) I'm almost embarrassed of my 41-year, total obsession with this guy, but never embarrassed enough not to talk about him when someone brings up his name. So with that, favorite solo album? Tough one ... In no particular order:
1. *Something/Anything*
2. *A Wizard, A True Star*
3. *Liars*

JVO: As far as (Rundgren-led band) Utopia goes, what's your favorite? I've always leaned towards *Oblivion*, which puts me in a minority.

BS: Whoa, another tough one. Two-way tie this time, in no particular order:
1. *Todd Rundgren's Utopia*; a Prog-rock masterpiece.
2. *Utopia*; a New Wave masterpiece.

And I'm right there with you on *Oblivion*. Love it! Great record. Kasim Sulton's favorite Utopia song is on that album, "I Will Wait," while I'm a fan of "Welcome To My Revolution."

JVO: While on the Utopia topic, I also think that "Trapped" from *Oops Wrong Planet* is one of the best songs ever.

BS: "Trapped" is indeed classic Todd/Utopia. Lots to like on that album as well, including the very ethereal "Windows" sung by Roger Powell and side two's "My Angel." Great chord changes in that one!

JVO: If a space alien landed here wanting to learn about rock and roll, which era, scene, or movement would you encourage the alien to start investigating?

BS: I'd have to direct E.T. to rock's beginnings. That's always been the most fascinating era to me simply because of the clash of cultures that erupted into rock and roll in the first place.

Steve Dahl, one of modern radio's true pioneers, has long been a favorite of mine. After being bounced around different dayparts (loosely speaking, showtimes) at two of Chicago's most bottom-feeding stations, WCKG and WJMK, he was yanked from the air in 2008.

(December 7, 2008)

<u>Steve Dahl</u>

I posted and quickly pulled down a post about Steve Dahl's morning show on 10/28/08. I didn't love the way it was written, so I made a mental note to edit and repost it at some point. Since Dahl got cut loose by JACK on Friday, I decided to repost my original thoughts, revision-free:

In my current career role, I don't have the need to meticulously observe radio ratings. I don't know who's up a tenth, down a tenth, or struggling with such things as "non-ethnic men over 18."

As such, I don't have a complete read on how Steve Dahl's migration to JACK-FM has impacted the station.

(Lamentedly) former Sun-Times columnist Rob Feder spelled out a dark PPM world where Dahl occupies a subterranean spot normally reserved for brokered and college radio.

If that's true, it's a real shame. Dahl's been doing consistently solid radio since jumping frequencies and dayparts. When he's at his best, his humor and topics come across as natural and effortless, something other mic jockeys forcing yuks up and down the dial could (and should, really) learn from.

The real secret to Dahl is the very secret to radio's survival--his show is hyperlocal. Dahl strikes a chord through shared regional experience. When he talks about walking down Michigan Avenue in shorts on a cold day or a candle shop in Bolingbrook, he's relating in a way a syndicated host never can. What's more, the show's been bare-bones when I've been listening. Without the morning show wacky whistles and bells that have become so tired and so cliche, Dahl's show stands as authentic, intelligent, and appealingly local.

The threat of satellite radio to terrestrial stations seemed very real for a while. The idea of deeper and more narrow channels, along with the endorsement of radio titan Howard Stern, made a lot of broadcasters nervous.

And then...

(January 27, 2009)

Sirius XM

Sirius XM needs to pay 175 million in debt by February 17th in order to stay afloat. Staring at that unreachable goal, the satellite radio company hired advisers to start getting things in motion for a Chapter 11 filing. While a buyout by Echostar or some similar cash-rich glutton-for-punishment is possible, I think we can all agree that the satellite experiment is near the end.

Less than seven months after Sirius and XM merged, the situation couldn't look more bleak. The current stock price is sitting at seven cents a share, which suddenly makes terrestrial radio stocks look like licenses to print money.

The funny thing is, I never subscribed to satellite radio. Not because I was towing some sort of solidarity line for terrestrial radio; I simply couldn't justify paying for it. A radio station (or in this case, collection of channels) would have to make me breakfast every day and hand deliver my weekly comic books in order for me to consider paying for the privilege to hear it. Howard Stern? Not a fan. And for those moments when I need truly avant garde and niche programming, I can always count on my iPod, as heard through 87.9 on my car's FM band. I don't care how exciting, challenging, insert-synonym-here, satellite radio's playlists are, you just can't beat the joy of hearing "Grace Kelly" by Mika segue into "Countess Bathory" by Venom, as I did on my way home from work tonight.

The fact that Sirius XM has amassed this much debt should surprise no one. Before the merger, both Sirius and XM spent vast and conspicuous amounts of money to make people aware of the concept of satellite radio and to brand themselves as "the" satellite provider. Furthermore, both were engaged in a twisted and high-priced content arms race, where obnoxious figures were thrown at talent and brands just to stay competitive. In the time it took you to read this far, Howard Stern made more money than you'll make this year. See what I mean?

And how niche does America really want its programming to be? We're talking about a country that allowed Nickelback and American Idol to dominate the musical tastes of the 21st century's opening years. Ours is not a culture hungering to be challenged. I'm sure that the Bluegrass, Canadian Soft Rock, and Faction ("The Music of Action Sports") channels are unlike anything you can find on terrestrial radio. I'm also sure that I'd rather eat glass than listen to any of them.

After taking a hard look at talent contracts, the biggest financial issue for Sirius XM is likely the core of their business--the satellites themselves. This is a company whose livelihood is dependent on things that are orbiting in outer-fucking-space. I'm no rocket scientist, but I've got to think that maintaining satellites and that level of technology doesn't come cheap.

While I'm indifferent to the idea of satellite radio going away, the possibility that yet even more broadcasters are facing the possibility of being "beached" in this unforgiving economy makes my stomach hurt. It's enough to get me rooting for a Sirius XM bailout.

When you're in radio, you have to accept the idea that you will get fired at some point; it's never a question of "if."

I'd been lucky for most of my career. I went from 1994 through most of 2005 without losing a job. And then came the day when ABC Radio, parent company of WZZN (The Zone) pulled the plug on the Active Rock format.

I'll never forget the day: September 25, 2005. I was on the air doing my midday show when I was summoned from studio into the station conference room. "But, my show..." I said. "What about my show?"

"We've got it covered," I was told.

As I approached the conference room, I noticed that the blinds were completely drawn around it. When I walked in, I saw the Program Director, Assistant Program Director, and General Manager, and fellow air personalities. There was also an unfamiliar person in the room, who I quickly discovered was an HR rep from the "home office."

We were fired en masse minutes after I walked into the room.

(October 1, 2005)

<u>On the Beach</u>

Fired. Toast. Shitcanned. Sayonara. And that was my Monday.

The good news is, if you're going to be "terminated," there's no better time than the beginning of Autumn. I mean, really, the Fall foliage around town is stunning.

In theory, I should've spent the past few days begging, pandering, and bribing my way into a new job. In theory.

I think anyone else who's been through the "we no longer need your services" rap would agree that a few days of not-thinking-about-the-industry decompression is the way to go. I haven't done anything close to productive since 11:35a.m.on Monday. Hang on, I take that back. I have done a ton of laundry. Just because I'm unemployed doesn't mean I shouldn't maintain my steadfast commitment to clean underpants.

After a couple weeks of unemployment, I fell victim to suffocating waves of stress and self-doubt. While unemployed, the important thing to maintain is a sense of humor, which became more challenging for me to do with each new day.

(October 12, 2005)

<u>Contemplating My Future</u>

The thing about working in radio is that, when you're unemployed, you start to wonder if you have any other marketable skills. Imagine my horror when I realized I don't. I've talked with a few stations, and things look good, though I'm totally open to pulling down a 20 hour a week barista job at Starbucks. Great benefits, free Antigone Rising CD's, whole bean coffee to take home–it's not a regular airshift, by any means, but I s'pose it's something regular.

I was unemployed until January, 2006, when Q101 hired me back to do overnights (midnight-5:30 a.m.).

Four months into the job, my wife and I had our second child.
The challenges that came with working those (fucking awful)
hours while raising a newborn and a toddler were emotionally
exhausting and physically debilitating. Despite that, I was ecstatic
to be working, even more so to be back at the station I started my
career at.

In July, 2006, Q101 parted ways with long-time morning man
and megatalent, Mancow Muller. As they searched for his
replacement, I held down morning drive on an interim basis. The
official name of my temporary show was the ridiculous "Summer
of Shuffle." Because our playlist was like an iPod. On Shuffle.
Get it?

My show wasn't much of a "show;" I was mandated to play a
shitload of songs every hour. I did get to interview a bunch of
bands, though, so I managed to have fun in the process.

Being "the guy in the chair" the first day on the air after
Mancow was shown the door was…rough.

(July 16, 2006)

Morning Drive: Day One

It's 5:30 in the morning, 30 minutes before "The Summer
of Shuffle" begins. Change does not come without growing
pains. I got a call on the request line last week that was sorta
chilling: "So, I hear Mancow's leaving."
"Yes, that's true," I said.
"I heard yer a faggot."
Click.

Only a year and a half after I'd been fired by the Zone, I got 86'd by Q101. On 4/20/07, at 5:30 in the morning, I was cut loose from my overnight gig to make way for a kid who was new-to-radio (the talented Kevin Manno, who rocketed up to MTV in 2010).

I was done with radio at that point. I just couldn't imagine going through the stress and humiliation of looking for another radio job, to say nothing of eventually losing another radio job. I swore I'd never again put my family through that nightmare.

"Never again" lasted for 2 ½ years. I rejoined Q101 in a part-time capacity in August, 2009. Old habits die hard.

FINAL THOUGHTS

As I worked on the final edits of this manuscript, all I could think was, "holy hell, this may be the most self-indulgent thing I've ever done."

If in reading this collection, you found any enjoyment, forced a smile, or landed on a topic you wanted to discuss or debate, I've exceeded my own expectations.

Thanks again.

ABOUT THE AUTHOR

James VanOsdol is a Chicago-based media personality who's been heard on major stations WKQX-FM (Q101), WZZN-FM (The Zone) , WXRT-FM (93XRT), and WLUP-FM (The Loop). He's been an active blogger since 2004, and regularly blogs on his own site (jamesvanosdol.com).

He listens to a lot of music and reads a lot of science fiction, horror, and comic books.

This is his first book, and hopefully not his last.